MW00513886

RULES THAT GUIDE US

Creating Stability During Uncertain Times

Glenn J. Mendoza, M.D.
Dawn M. Myers

UNICORN LIGHT
PUBLISHING

ISBN: 978-0-9859708-5-7

Request for permission to reproduce selections
from this book should be mailed to:
Unicorn Light Publishing Company
420 Valley Brook Avenue
Lyndhurst, New Jersey 07071

RULES THAT GUIDE US

Creating Stability During Uncertain Times

Glenn J. Mendoza, M.D.
Dawn M. Myers

UNICORN LIGHT
PUBLISHING

Dedication

We affectionately dedicate this work to our beloved teacher, GrandMaster Choa Kok Sui, and his great teacher, Mahaguruji Mei Ling: For your love, blessings, healings, guidance, wisdom, and inspiration. May your teachings, compassion, and light continue to heal and transform people's lives around the world.

And to all the participants of the 100-day meditation and to all men and women who regularly practice the Meditation on Twin Hearts: We believe our efforts are surely making this world a better place.

We also dedicate this work to:

My sons Asa, Kris, and Edel:
Our family's rules emerged from embodying the values of love, respect, honesty, humor, and harmony. My heart warms to see those same values continue as you parent your own children.

My grandchildren Hope, Leo, Vera, Teo, and Cara:
Marilag and I adore you more than you will ever know. There are no rules for a grandparents' love. Always keep that infinite love within your heart.

Glenn J. Mendoza

My Mom and Dad:
Thank you for encouraging me to follow my inner compass. Your greatest gift to me was how you loved me and allowed me to be who I am. I am grateful to know I always have your unconditional love and support. Everything you did (and did not do) was perfect.

My sons Jack and Mark:
May you find great happiness, purpose, and meaning while following your own inner compass. I will always love and support you in all that you do. Remember: your love can change the world.

Dawn M. Myers

Table of Contents

Preface

Navigating the journey of life can take us down many unfamiliar paths. The roads we encounter may vary, but the forward movement we each experience has similarities. As the two of us reflected on this together, we realized we wanted to write a set of rules that could serve as guidelines to help create more stability during these uncertain times and to encourage all of us to see beyond the surface of our struggles.

We could not have successfully completed this book without a strong support group for whom we are very grateful. Our family supported us with love and understanding, as did the thousands of meditators who joined us each night – each of whom has provided us with support, inspiration, and feedback throughout.

The rules in this book emerged during profound moments of silence. They gently guided us forward as the whisper of our souls told us that everything would be alright. Together, we emerged with greater wisdom, clarity, and kindness because of the time we spent together. The idea for writing a book of these rules emerged during those memorable evenings.

Ultimately, we hope that *Rules That Guide Us* can serve as a guidebook to redirect our focus from the external, help us look within, and use these challenging times as an inspiration to create greater depth, meaning, and purpose in our lives.

Glenn J. Mendoza, M.D.
Dawn M. Myers

Foreword

In 2020, many of us turned inward as we remained isolated at home, separated from much that we loved and needed. For some, this inward journey turned into a blessing, but for many more, it turned into a hardship that was almost beyond endurance.

The insecurity, uncertainty, and grief turned many people upside down and inside out. True North – that still center of morality and being within us – eluded many. Even as the crisis lifts, some continue to struggle. Still others have seen tremendous spiritual growth. Many have banded together to help heal each other and the earth through meditation, intention, and community. They have deepened their levels of compassion and love.

So, what has helped to make the difference? Values have; finding one's moral center and inner light have; and learning and being guided by the right rules have.

We have all needed to learn about the "rules that guide us" in order to create stability in uncertain times. And we have needed someone very wise to show us the way.

What is it the Buddhists say? "When the student is ready, the teacher will appear." Well, for a very lucky number of us, that teacher would be Pranic Healer Master Glenn Mendoza, M.D. and Dawn Myers, co-authors of this glorious jewel of a book.

I was extremely lucky because on the day the pandemic officially was declared, my husband and I escaped from Manhattan to our home in Montauk, New York, unsettled but safe. That evening, a dear and spiritual friend dedicated to energy healing told me that his teacher had started a meditation group on Zoom each night at 8 p.m. It was free, global, and deeply centering; its goal was to help heal one another and the planet. He invited me to join. I did, and I think it saved my life.

For 100 days straight, thousands from around the world meditated together – doing the Meditation on Twin Hearts – and listened to Master Glenn guide us to become better, bigger, kinder, and more compassionate souls than we ever could have envisioned being. This was his gift to the world – and us.

I, along with so many others, found it powerful beyond belief, and I have integrated meditation and healing into my "new normal" life. Master Glenn's and Dawn's wisdom is profound, simple, and an amalgam of some of the best spiritual practices from around the world. And we need it here and now.

I believe we all need it. As the saying dictates: we are ready, and this wonderful book has appeared. It is for you. Enjoy. And thank you, Master Glenn.

Davia B. Temin
President and CEO
Temin and Company Incorporated

"During any time of disorientation in life, it is essential to identify and travel towards our "true north," our internal moral compass, a fixed point that is unique to each person."

Introduction

In mid-March 2020, many retreated to their homes in light of the looming global outbreak of a coronavirus pandemic. Overwhelmed with fear and uncertainty, public officials called for a lockdown and instructed everyone to stay at home. So we did, awaiting the unknown. As the world began to experience drastic shifts in their daily lives, everyone was faced with a unique and unexpected experience.

As fear and uncertainty grew worldwide, the authors initiated a global Meditation on Twin Hearts. The intention was to use this unique and powerful practice of metta, or "loving-kindness," meditation to address the stress, anxiety, and fears that many people were experiencing. We originally expected that the group meditation would last for just seven evenings, but it grew into a hundred nights. And while we started with several hundred meditators, the size of the group grew to thousands of people from many different countries, religions, and philosophies, gathering nightly to take refuge from the emerging fear.

At first, the nightly meditations felt like a retreat; the group helped each of us calm our fears and created a sense of stability in the face of current events. As the evenings passed, however, our inner states strengthened, and we began to experience a deeper sense of transformation and more profound openings of our hearts. As our nerves calmed, we blessed Mother Earth with the seeds of hope, love, and healing that the world desperately needed. Together we grew and merged our inner worlds together and began to experience a collective state – one of profound inner stillness, inner peace, and for some oneness. As our eyes opened to the deep transformation happening within, we focused our attention on the emerging internal awareness – even as the external world crisis continued to unfold.

During any time of disorientation in life, it is essential to identify and travel towards our "true north," our internal moral compass, a fixed point that is unique to each person. Those who successfully navigated the unchartered waters of 2020 with any sense of clarity or calmness had to align themselves to their own true north. Like the GPS we use in our cars, fixing our focus on a set direction helps us move forward when we're traveling in unknown lands. When we align with our true north, we can relax and trust the journey as we head forward with our eyes set on what matters most.

For many of us, our nightly Meditation on Twin Hearts became our true north during those uncertain times.

One of the authors (GJM) gave short talks before the meditations each night to help strengthen our minds to better understand the transformation we were collectively experiencing. We shined the light of awareness on our experience, and we learned, grew, and ultimately moved forward together. From those nightly lectures, certain universal truths began to emerge, anchoring an understanding that seemed to dissolve barriers of time and space. Both authors received thousands of emails from people who wanted to share their meditations and personal experiences, their stories of inspirations, poems, miraculous healings, insights, clarity, reflections, and endless gratitude.

Throughout all of our time together, seeds of fellowship bloomed. Inner transformation took a stronger hold. We began to see beyond the situation we found ourselves in and began to understand that the truths – or rules – that we were unearthing could act as a foundation for us as we journey forward and face other challenging times in the future.

This book is a collection of the rules, insights, and action steps of our journey through 2020. Our intention for writing this book is to highlight the silver linings – the hope, inspiration, and growth we experienced as a group at that moment in time and space. We believe these rules can be used as guideposts for anyone's journey forward.

In addition to the rules, a sweetness and a loving energy emerged, reflecting the time we spent together, and we found comfort in our daily practice, our spiritual growth, and the collective bond we created during the global coronavirus pandemic of 2020.

100 Days of Meditation

Learning directly from such a great spiritual teacher as GrandMaster Choa Kok Sui was a unique opportunity. Over the years, he was asked many challenging questions; some were simple, and some were very complex. The responses he gave were always unique, eye-opening, and deeply insightful. There were times when he would pause, look upward, and respond with a simple, "Let me meditate on it."

This simple act of acknowledging the need for deeper reflection is itself a gift that allows for greater insight when the mind does not have an immediate answer. When the coronavirus pandemic began, and everyone was faced with all sorts of uncertainties, we knew instinctively that we needed to meditate in order to gain a deeper understanding of the emerging events and to get more clarity about how those events would uniquely affect each of us.

GrandMaster Choa Kok Sui, the modern founder of Pranic Healing and Arhatic Yoga, is a spiritual teacher who introduced The Meditation on Twin Hearts as a gift to humanity. He simplified very advanced spiritual teachings into a system of energy healing and spiritual growth that is easy to understand and implement. His teachings are taught around the world in many different languages, religions, and cultures. His powerful impact, along with his books, courses, and meditations, continues to transform lives.

The Meditation on Twin Hearts is just one of his many powerful gifts. It is unique in that it activates the energy centers of the heart and crown. In turn, we experience greater love and compassion for those around us as well as a deeper sense of love for all of humanity. It is also known to help relax and calm the mind and evoke feelings of hope and peace. Scientific studies have validated these findings. The authors felt that, during these times, it was exactly what all of us needed individually, as a community, and in the world at large.

As a group, we journeyed through 100 consecutive days of meditations. In light of the global crisis, we created a haven of peace, transformation, hope, and joy. We each had our own path and own experiences, but the guiding light we followed was the same.

How to Use this Book

We recommend that you first read *Rules That Guide Us* cover to cover, but you can use the book as a reference as well. You can jump right to the sections that you resonate with during times of need. Uncertainty comes at different moments in our lives, affects us in a variety of ways, and lasts for any length of time. We might find ourselves in a period of instability for a day or two or for weeks, months, a year, or possibly even more. Regardless, we are all touched by times of change as long as we are alive and growing on this beautiful planet Earth. This book can help with those moments.

Our intention for this book is to provide you with some guidance, clarity, and, ultimately, strength as you navigate your own uncharted waters. You might be experiencing a major physical change in health, or you might be at the end of a relationship. Or perhaps you're experiencing a breakup, a divorce, a move, a transition, or a change in your job. Sewn into all of these changes is the thread of unfamiliarity. Because they can sometimes be intense and jarring to your sense of well-being, it is important to strengthen your inner world to help you navigate the change with intention.

Each chapter focuses on a positive quality, value, or virtue that we need to strengthen within ourselves. As we navigate times of change, there are certain patterns to our forward movement, and the chapters of this book are intended to mirror those patterns. In each chapter, we present five rules followed by points for inner reflection and firm resolution, statements of gratitude, and, finally, statements of affirmation. All of them are offered as invitations to spark ideas of hope and inspiration, provoke deeper awareness, and bring greater clarity into your world. As we develop and strengthen new perspectives and insights, we claim them as part of our new thought process and nourish them as future patterns.

Action Steps

Inner Reflection and Firm Resolution:
Cleansing and Programming the Mind

Many of us have heard that, at the end of our lives, there is a "review" – a period where our lives pass before our eyes or consciousness, and we become aware of the positive and negative aspects of our thoughts and actions. As a response to that, GrandMaster Choa Kok Sui introduced and taught his students the practice of Inner Reflection and Firm Resolution – a technique to increase awareness. Thus, as we learn to review our lives on a daily basis, we experience new opportunities for growth and change.

Master Choa, as his students fondly called him, recommended that upon waking up in the morning or at the end of each day, we spend 10 to 15 minutes reviewing and reflecting upon our thoughts, feelings, and actions of the previous 24 hours. If there were discomforts or unhappy exchanges, we have the opportunity to be aware of and identify the patterns of thought that generated the unwanted action. This process increases our awareness and builds the "muscle" within our minds to act with more intention in the future.

Lord Buddha taught three levels of awareness. First: Upon reflection, you become aware that the words you spoke earlier were harsh. Second: You become aware of the negative words as you say them. Third: You become aware of the negative thoughts before you say them, so you don't say them at all.

Being aware of our thoughts and changing our behavior before we act is our ultimate goal.

The Practice of Inner Reflection and Firm Resolution

When we identify unwanted actions we want to work on, we can erase or disintegrate their memory or pattern. Master Choa taught us to put three fingers of the left hand – thumb, pointer, and middle finger – into the energy center at the space between the eyebrows while simultaneously using the right hand to intentionally and energetically "erase" the unwanted thoughts or actions or pattern of behavior. In other words, while your left fingers are between your eyebrows, move your right hand in a side-to-side motion, erasing the memories in your mind.

Once we have erased an unwanted behavior, we can make a firm resolution to correct the mistakes of the day by mentally creating a thought or image about how we would have wanted to respond. This is our opportunity to insert the right thoughts, right speech, and right actions into our experience. We replace and reprogram the mind to act according to our desired outcome. As we do this, it is essential that we see the resolution clearly and that we use our will to imbue the experience with the positive properties we're choosing. This balance is vital as we move forward in a positive direction.

Incorporating the practice of Inner Reflection and Firm Resolution into your daily life can bring tremendous emotional and spiritual development. In each chapter, we offer suggestions to help the process and to help spawn ideas if you ever feel stuck. Ultimately, practicing Inner Reflection and Firm Resolution can greatly increase your awareness when focused on your personal life experience and the actions you want to transform. Master Choa said that when we become more aware of our behaviors, we begin to realize that our thoughts are the seeds and our feelings, words, and actions are the fruits. Whether we are aware of it or not, ultimately, it all starts with our thoughts. Practicing Inner Reflection and Firm Resolution addresses the underlying thoughts that are the precursors to our actions.

Gratitude to Open the Heart

Gratitude opens the heart and helps us infuse our lives with more love and appreciation. When we live in a state of gratitude, we shift into a place of appreciation and abundance. Often, we view life with a filter of what we want to change and how we might improve, but this mindset reflects a sense of lack and not being good enough. Without any physical change in our outer experience, gratitude shifts our perceptions so that we see that what we currently have is not only enough; it is everything we need. Gratitude fills our beings with positive feelings of thankfulness. Suddenly, our lives are not lacking; they are overflowing with blessings.

In the Gratitudes section of each chapter, we offer suggestions to infuse our lives with gratitude according to the topic. Read them and practice experiencing the feelings of gratitude and appreciation towards these areas in your life. Certain phrases might stand out to you at certain times, and you might want to focus on one more than others. Ultimately, your gratitude practice will become a unique personalized experience, but feel free to use our suggestions as a foundation to move forward.

Affirmations to Strengthen the Will

Affirmations plant seeds of positive new perspectives for us to live by. The thoughts we think repetitively get incorporated into our conscious and unconscious minds and can be felt in our emotional patterns and affect our well-being. If we can replace some of our negative thinking with positive affirmations, our brain, nervous system, and automatic thinking will shift to positivity and optimism.

We offer several suggestions for affirmations within each chapter topic and recommend that you read and recite them often. At first, the affirmations might feel conceptual, but eventually, you will begin to experience them in your body as well. Some of them might stand out more than others, depending on what you feel you need at that time. Try to recall and repeat one affirmation or several of them throughout the day until you begin to feel that it has become a natural expression for you.

Our suggestions might inspire ideas for additional affirmations that are specific to your situation. Go ahead and use affirmations that feel right for the situation you're in and those that feel like they can help you begin to fulfill your goals.

Three Rules to Get Started

Welcome new ideas with an open mind and a grateful heart.

Open your mind and heart to the wisdom held within these pages. These rules were written with love and with the intention to help you along your journey of life. Not every idea will resonate with you in the current moment but open your heart and read it anyway. At a deeper level, these concepts are planting seeds for future ideas to grow. How can one progress and learn if one is not open? A narrow or closed mind can find something wrong with almost anything. On the other hand, an open mind and a grateful heart will always find something positive in everything.

Growth happens in layers. Honor each phase.

Where we are and where we want to be can be two very different places. We encourage you to be patient and take the necessary steps to move yourself forward. Jumping ahead prematurely can result in an unstable foundation that cannot support the progress you want to jump ahead to. Engage in all the small steps and celebrate the smaller levels of increased awareness as they are building the foundation you need to move forward. The more emotional, physical, and spiritual stability you have in each layer will contribute to the end result you're ultimately seeking.

Carry forward the concepts that resonate with your growth.

In life, we can often be presented with many ideas. Our interest in them is the first level of truth for us, our understanding of them is another level, and whether or not we accept them into our hearts is even a deeper level of truth. Take with you and carry forward only those truths that resonate in your heart. Tuck away any ideas that do not seem relevant at the moment and feel free to let go of those that do not resonate at all. The guidance you need will stand out at those times in your life when it is meant to be incorporated to support you through issues you face. Then, be aware of the rules that leave an indelible mark and open your heart to inspire positive action – and take them with you. Use them and incorporate them your life. Practice them with patience, master them with your mind, and live your life with love.

In conclusion, we hope that, within these pages, you find a door that opens and leads you to your own inner wisdom and guidance. Your journey might have similarities with the journeys of others, but you will ultimately navigate and grow in your own unique way.

We hope that our words spark a light of hope in your heart and positive thoughts in your mind and that they nurture a deep sense of joy in your soul. We hope they serve as a guiding hand to help you navigate your own inner and outer journey through whatever path of uncertainty you might encounter.

Read with a light heart and a clear mind. Trust that, just as you've found your way to this book, you will find the guidance you seek within its pages. Some rules might resonate more than others, and some might call out more at different times. Whatever your situation, we hope you find comfort in these pages and allow the love in which they were written to touch and uplift your heart and mind.

You are not alone as you journey on your unique and unfamiliar path.

CHANGE

Change can pave roads to destinations we've
dreamed of but did not know how to get to.

*Those who don't want to change,
let them sleep.*

~ Rumi

CHANGE

Every great journey, every transition, and every new decision embodies aspects of change. We cannot avoid change and create something new at the same time. Change itself is neutral; the ways we react to what is changing reflect our inner world and our ability to adapt to the unknown. When we lean into trusting that life will unfold for our highest good, it can carry us to places we never thought possible. Change can pave roads to destinations we've dreamed of but did not know how to get to.

Our first reaction to change is often fear and uncertainty. We fear because we feel a lack of control and because we don't know what will result from the new situation. Our mind begins the exhausting and endless task of attempting to make sense of situations that have not yet happened. In effect, we cling to the familiarity of the current situation and fear the unknown of future situations.

People will often stay in a job where they are unhappy or unsatisfied because they fear change. Their minds are filled with numerous possibilities of what could go wrong because changing jobs holds so many uncertainties. The mind will explore endless possibilities as it tries to find some peace with an outcome that it can understand and that we can feel comfortable with. But the truth is, we have a choice of whether we project our fears or our hopes into the future. This same person could seek a new job and fill their minds with hope for greater opportunities, new relationships, new growth, and professional exposure.

Every day offers possibilities of change and opportunities for the unknown to find its way into our comfort zones. Once we see the purpose and the gift that change offers us, we can lean in and trust the process to move us forward to experiences we might not have been able to get on our own. Our lack of faith will begin to fade.

By embracing change, we can begin the journey from where we are to where we want to be.

Rule 1
Change is the bridge we must cross to create something new in our lives.

Many of us have dreams and desires for our lives to be better and different than they are. We can envision the end result but not the process to get us there. Change is part of that process. It is difficult to create something new while staying exactly the same. Things usually need to shift, break down, and alter to allow new things to open up and come into our lives. Embracing the process of change is like walking across a bridge; we are leaving what was and walking towards what could be.

Rule 2
The first step is the hardest, but each step gets easier.

Change is constantly happening, but how much we participate in it depends on our ability to accept it and step forward through it. Some people stay in denial, rejection, fear, or blame; they withdraw, or they just observe what is happening from afar. Yet making the decision to step forward and be part of a new journey engages us with the possibilities that can result from the change. To fully embrace what is happening in our lives, we must take that first step; only then can we reap the benefits. With faith and no fear, take the first step.

Rule 3
Embrace the unexpected.

While life rarely unfolds exactly the way we want it to, unexpected shifts can create space for something bigger, stronger, and more powerful to come into our lives. Embracing the unexpected is accepting that life is made up of things we can control and things that we cannot. If we can learn to embrace the unexpected instead of resisting it, we can embark on a path that can lead us to greater gifts, even if we don't see those gifts at first glance.

Rule 4
Don't "go with the flow." *Be* the flow.

It can be easy to be swayed by other people's opinions and expectations, especially during times of great change and uncertainty. At these times, it is important to go within, get clarity, strengthen the qualities you believe to be true for you, and stand grounded in how you want to interact with the world. Find a way to dance between expressing who you truly are and finding peace with what life brings you. Create your own flow and go at your own pace. After all, we always have the ability to choose how we react to life.

Rule 5
Tough times do not last forever.

There is a rule of cycles that states: difficult times will not last forever. We have to move forward and begin to create the life we want, even as we experience change and discomfort. Otherwise, we might find ourselves waiting forever for the "right" time or situation. As difficult as things might seem right now, by the law of change, it will pass, and things will get easier. Continue living your life and know that it will not remain as it is forever.

INNER REFLECTION & FIRM RESOLUTION:
Reflect:
- In what areas of my life am I currently experiencing a time of change?
- Have I stepped forward to embrace the change, or am I just observing?
- What are my most common, recurring negative or limiting thoughts at this time?

Erase:
- Any negative thoughts about yourself or thoughts that are directed at others as a result of things changing.
- Any fears of what could go wrong.
- Any limiting beliefs that make you feel small or stuck.

Visualize:
- Things unfolding with ease and grace.
- A happy outcome.
- A positive balance to the negative thoughts that were erased.

GRATITUDES:

I am grateful for this new opportunity.
I am grateful for my strengths.
I am grateful for my support.
I am grateful for all that is going right in life.
I am grateful for the change I am experiencing.

AFFIRMATIONS:

My life is unfolding as it should.
I am strong enough to weather this phase of change.
Calmer days are ahead.
Amazing gifts will result from this time.
I am stronger because of this experience.

PAUSE

Pause is an opportunity to create space between
what is happening and our reaction to it.

*Move, but don't move the way
fear makes you move.*

~ Rumi

PAUSE

Just as caterpillars cocoon, when we pause, we withdraw. We halt our patterned behaviors to create something new. A pause enables the cocooning that provides the void for transformation. In this withdrawal state, we might experience a variety of emotions, and we might go even deeper into powerful states of inner reflection. This radical process is necessary for the caterpillar to eventually transform and emerge as a butterfly.

The ways that most people react in life are based on patterned behaviors — behaviors that are conditioned, predictable, and often mechanical and automatic. Like computer programs, the life experiences that have been coded into our lives will play out through our reactions. This default programming is embedded in our subconscious minds. If we have experienced a lot of judgment, criticism, and anger from others in our lives, we will react to life similarly. If we have experienced a lot of love, joy, and understanding, we will react to life in that way.

Transformation is possible when we pause and realize we are able to avoid, resist, and release our habitual patterns and reprogram ourselves to react in a way that is more aligned with the truth of who we are.

We can create small pauses in our lives with quiet walks, meditations, or calm breathing and, by doing so, give ourselves opportunities to replenish our energy and increase our awareness. Otherwise, life might hand us a pause of its own, a break in our regular routine, perhaps in the form of an illness, or some even more drastic change to our daily life.

A common pause people experience is a vacation. It is an intentional pause from our everyday patterns of work and homelife. People stop their regular activities and seek out new and foreign experiences to relax their patterned behaviors and stimulate new emotions and expressions of self. After a pleasurable pause such as this, people return feeling renewed and refreshed. If we remain partially connected to emails and working some of the time, we may not experience the depth of re-set that a deep, true pause can offer.

Our goal during times of pause is to shed unwanted patterns and emotions. As we remain aware, we can allow them to release and choose a reaction that is more aligned with our growth. Like a muscle that needs to be constantly exercised, we need to practice pausing to be able to endure our ongoing development. Doing so ultimately gives us a healthy awareness and control over how we engage in the world. Then we can look at the world with new eyes, a renewed awareness, to see and accept what we have become in the world that is waiting for us.

Rule 6
Embrace the pause!

To embrace the pauses in our lives, we must honor what is being given to us. We are used to moving through life at a certain speed, and when life suddenly shifts and changes, our natural reaction might be to keep up the pace but take new action. When we do that, we are not embracing the pause, just shifting our focus. The process of slowing and allowing pauses to fully bloom in life can help us develop new perspectives and, ultimately, new paths. Use the time of change to review where you are, how you feel, where you want to go and what changes can be implemented in the process.

Rule 7
The gap between action and reaction is sacred ground.

There is tremendous power in controlling our reactions to life. In order to maintain emotional clarity and not instantly react to something, we must first pause. When we pause our emotions and thoughts, we can bring awareness to what is happening, discern if we are just reacting out of habit or programming, and choose to act in a way we'd prefer. This pause or gap in our reactions can be the sacred ground on which we claim our life as our own.

Rule 8
Small pauses can create big change.

We often overlook the power of making small adjustments along our path. Small decisions, such as pausing to bring awareness to our breath, slowing down to meditate daily, taking a walk in nature, journaling, or ending the day with gratitude, can be seen as small pauses in our day. When done regularly, these small actions can change the entire direction of our lives. Find moments to pause and create small adjustments to your path.

Rule 9
Be aware without judgment or expectations.

Be aware before you assume that certain situations will cause certain reactions. We often believe that we need to be sad when someone passes away or that we will be angry when we have been wronged. But this is not always the case. The pauses we take in our journey through change offer an opportunity for reflection and awareness. Refrain from judgment or expectations, such as: "I should be happy" or "I should be sad." These thoughts clutter the mind and blind it from seeing the truth of what you truly are feeling. Pause. Then tune into however you truly feel and allow whatever is there to come forth.

Rule 10
Breathe through the discomforts.

Relax and breathe into the discomforts of your current situation. A time of change is a process of growth and transformation, and there will be times that are smoother than others. Refrain from rushing or pushing; try to just breathe and relax into the process. Our emotions, our minds, and our mindsets are being stretched and developed. Not every phase will be enjoyable, but each part contributes to the whole. Remember: just breathe.

INNER REFLECTION & FIRM RESOLUTION:
Reflect:
- Do I create enough time and space for healthy pauses in my life?
- What thoughts and feelings arise when I slow down and pause?
- How do I respond to myself? Am I positive or negative in my self-talk?

Erase:
- Negative feelings or thoughts about giving yourself time and space to pause.
- Any self-judgment.
- Any excuses that prevent pauses.

Visualize:
- That you have plenty of time to pause and reflect.
- Enjoying the time and space between actions and events in your life.
- A positive balance to the negative thoughts that were erased.

GRATITUDES:

I am grateful for my breath and the space it creates.
I am grateful for my mind and its ability to change pace.
I am grateful for the minor adjustments I make in my life.
I am grateful for all unexpected turns of events.
I am grateful for the pauses in my life.

AFFIRMATIONS:

I allow space in my busy schedule for pause.
I accept time to be without having to be busy.
I allow the time of pause to bring new things into my life.
Pause is a gift of redirection.
I embrace the gift of pausing.

FAITH

Faith is when we are in the heart of our struggles, but keep our eyes focused on the possible benefits that might come from it.

*Prayers change from religion to religion.
But faith is always the same.*

~ Rumi

FAITH

Faith is complete trust and confidence that life is unfolding for our best interest. How do we know things will be OK? Like a newborn baby who trusts that everything will be provided for, we can trust that life or the Universe will provide and give us exactly what we need — even if it's not what we want at the moment. As much as we think we know what we want, our desires are often based on what we think we can handle more than what is in our best interest to develop and grow.

When we have faith, we trust that life will unfold for our highest good — which might not always be for our highest comfort.

When we face challenging times, it can be difficult to feel confident that things are unfolding in our favor. If things are not good right now, how can we believe things will be better in the future? Faith is the ability to believe that what is happening is divinely guided even if we don't yet see how. It might feel like everything is falling apart and our lives seem to be unraveling, but the change at hand might actually be making room for new and better things to come.

For example, when we have a broken heart, the pain might seem unbearable. Our emotions feel raw, our thoughts get disconnected, and our outlook is bleak. It might be difficult to find something positive to focus on since everything seems painful at the moment. But we eventually heal and move forward, and we might meet someone new and find deeper levels of love, happiness, and joy. We would then look back on the heartbreak and realize that it was necessary to get to where we are now. We can feel gratitude for the lessons learned.

Times of pain can help crack us open to deeper feelings of compassion, self-love, and clarity.

One gift that comes from living with faith is optimism. If we align with the possibility of negative outcomes, we will feel and attract that energy. If we align with faith, we will feel and attract the qualities of hope, positive emotions, positive outcomes, and infinite possibilities. Faith changes our whole being and helps to create the future we want by experiencing the positive possibilities in the present. One cannot be miserable and crave a positive life at the same time. We can feel and embody the optimism of faith so that life will unfold for our highest good.

Rule 11
Your heart is your compass.

The wisdom of the heart is our moral compass. When we go within and follow the wisdom in our hearts, we move forward with guidance that is infused with higher understandings. Our hearts generate higher frequencies of emotions, such as love, trust, faith, compassion, mercy, and hope, while our lower nature can reside in the negative emotions of fear, pain, anger, disappointment, regret, shame, and guilt. When we align our actions with our hearts, we tend to feel peace, calmness, and ease with our actions. Leaning into trusting these emotions connects us to a harmonious state that can ease our fears and loosen our illusion of control. This faith allows even more divine energy to guide us because we are not pushing against the unfolding but moving with it instead.

Rule 12
Look back to connect the dots.

When we look back on our paths, the steps we took make more sense to us because we can see the bigger picture. But when we look forward, we do not always understand where each step will lead us. In retrospect, we can see how the dots connected together, each step perfectly leading to the next, moving us forward to where we are now. As we observe these connections, we build confidence that life is supporting our best interests. It helps us build faith that, even though things might not be great right now, someday we will be able to reflect back on this period and appreciate it as a necessary part of the larger journey. Faith moves us forward even if each of our steps doesn't make sense yet. With faith, we believe that someday they will.

Rule 13
Surrender what is beyond control.

Surrender happens when we increase our inner receptivity to our higher nature. The word might give the impression of giving up or feeling defeated, but in truth, surrender is allowing a greater energy to move through us when we have tried everything ourselves. Surrendering is letting go of inner resistance and struggles and trusting that what is meant to be will be. This acceptance brings harmony into our lives, regardless of our expectations. True surrender is when we have faith and trust in how our life unfolds, confident that we will be supported in all outcomes.

Rule 14
We function with a higher purpose.

Having faith is relying on wisdom greater than our own. The force that moves us forward is called by many names, such as God, Universe, or Source. It silently weaves together the patterns of our collective lives into an image that is beyond our vision. Understanding that our lives are connected to this force infuses purpose and meaning to all of our daily actions. This mindset helps us to detach from our small struggles and see our lives as part of a larger and incomprehensible plan. Aligning our faith to this higher purpose allows us to hold steady on our paths.

Rule 15
When in doubt, meditate.

When our minds and emotions get overwhelmed and we crave deeper and higher wisdom, meditation becomes an act of surrender. It is an opportunity to calm the emotions, quiet the mind, and connect with greater awareness and faith. The process naturally flushes out lower emotions, creating space for new insights, clarity, and ideas. When you find yourself stuck, cycling through negative patterns, it is an ideal time to pause and seek inner stillness and inner peace through meditation. It is a great savior when needed but can also be practiced regularly to build inner strength to navigate through life with clarity and emotional balance.

INNER REFLECTION & FIRM RESOLUTION:

Reflect:
- Where do I have doubts or fears that interfere with my ability to trust and have faith that everything will be alright?
- Where do my negative thoughts overpower the positive when looking forward?
- What are my worries about the future?

Erase:
- Negative doubts and fears.
- Pessimistic thoughts and feelings.
- Any limiting beliefs that make you feel small and stuck.

Visualize:
- Everything will be alright.
- You are happy no matter how things unfold.
- A positive balance to the negative thoughts that were erased.

GRATITUDES:
I am grateful for my faith and trust that all will work out.
I am grateful that things work out with ease and grace.
I am grateful for the path of my forward movement.
I am grateful for my positive mindset.
I am grateful for all my blessings.

AFFIRMATIONS:
I am guided in all that I do.
Everything unfolds for my highest good.
I can see the blessings of my current situation.
Everything that is happening to me is helping me grow.
I am moving in the direction of my ultimate goal.

HOPE

Hope gives color and life to the formless faith.

Never lose hope.
Miracles always dwell in the invisible.

~ Rumi

HOPE

Hope is the creative aspect of faith. When we have faith, we believe things will work out aligned with a greater good or purpose. Hope gives color, life, and magic to faith. In this process, hope amplifies the possibilities by adding a silver lining, a rainbow at the end of the journey, an unexpected positive twist or turn. We end up attracting even more positive, happy thoughts and feelings when we have hope.

You might believe that life will turn out OK, but when you have hope, you believe life will be magnificent. Hope opens up possibilities that the outcome will be beautiful and better than we expected. It is a field of wildflowers, a sunset beyond our comprehension of beauty, a love deeper than we could have thought possible. Hope expands our minds past our expected outcomes. When life seems overwhelming or filled with darkness, we might sometimes find ourselves feeling hopeless and overwhelmed. When we feel cornered in life, we cannot see the possibilities or a positive way forward. This is where the gift of hope comes in. We might not be able to see the end result, but we can begin to work with what we have and move forward in whatever positive way possible.

An example of this is how people reacted during the coronavirus pandemic. As the world retreated into a lockdown, many people were feeling hopeless, uncertain, and overwhelmed with fear. A group of Pranic Healers gathered and organized Project Hope for Healing which provided Pranic Healing to those affected by COVID-19. As a result of this initial act of kindness, the organization gathered over 600 healers worldwide and provided more than 100,000 Pranic Healing sessions. They strengthened their community, provided service to global suffering, grew as healers, and developed a structure for future projects. At a time when all seemed lost and overwhelming, hope became another option for how the group moved forward.

Use whatever skills or talents you have to move forward with confidence that all will be well. Hope opens the door for greater inspiration and creativity. Hope turns a two-dimensional reality into a three-dimensional one; it turns a black and white situation into a colorful one; it turns our deepest despair into a yearning for something better. Hope awakens our senses, sparks inspiration, and pulls forth greater energy from within. When we live with hope, we live with optimism.

Rule 16
Appreciate beauty.

Beauty is one of the many facets of hope. When we feel hopeless, everything can seem dull and dark. Beauty in any form can brighten our situation and offer some light on a dull mindset. Seek activities that inspire beauty and hope. Look at beautiful pictures, go for a walk, read inspiring stories, connect with experiences that are uplifting to create these rays of sunshine on your thinking. As we see more possibilities of goodness in the world around us, we will see more possibilities of goodness in our own lives as well.

Rule 17
Offer hope to others.

Hope is a mindset and a state of being. When we are hopeful, we lift people up and create an environment of inspiration. Sometimes our own situations are the hardest to see hopeful possibilities in. Sharing rays of sunshine on others might come easier than being able to shine sunshine on yourself. Help to create and nurture other people's visions of hope and build your muscle of optimism. As you feel the possibilities and inspiration in others' lives, start to open and see the possibilities in your own life as well.

Rule 18
Make time for receiving.

During times of change, our minds can become laser-focused on enduring and making it to the other side of the challenges we face. Making time for receiving can invite softness into our experience. If we plow ahead with force, there is little room to receive insight, inspiration, or the possibility of new ideas. Being in a receptive state might mean having coffee with a friend, carving out some downtime, drawing, reflecting, meditating, walking, or writing. Many of us tend to give a lot of ourselves during times of change, so make sure you take time to receive as well.

Rule 19
Leave room for spontaneity.

Especially when we embark on a journey of change, we tend to cling to the familiar. But if our focus is fixed on our last threads of stability, we can miss unique opportunities presenting themselves to us. So, leave some space for spontaneity to show up on your journey. Hope for an unexpected turn of events. Do not get too hard or concrete in your thinking. We do not know how things will turn out, so stay open to any positive turn of events!

Rule 20
Keep the light of hope.

Life without hope is a life in darkness. Without hope, we get detached from living, and we lose the connection that ties us to possibilities that can move us forward. Keeping open the avenue of hope prevents us from giving up. It is essential to nurture these aspects of hope as it will be the very thing that keeps us moving forward in difficult times. Always keep the light of hope. There is no darkness that cannot be overcome with the light of hope.

INNER REFLECTION & FIRM RESOLUTION:
Reflect:
- What areas of my life feel gray and dull?
- How do I block or overlook opportunities for receiving and creativity?
- Where am I feeling hopeless?

Erase:
- Any thoughts or feelings that might hinder or block your ability to be hopeful.
- Any disbelief or negative thoughts about positive outcomes.
- Any limiting beliefs that make your future seem negative.

Visualize:
- A colorful, fantastic, and vibrant outcome!
- Infuse joy, happiness, and excitement into your ideas for the future.
- A positive balance to the negative thoughts that were erased.

GRATITUDES:
I am grateful for all the beauty in my life.
I am grateful for my avenues of creativity.
I am grateful for an open mind and an open heart.
I am grateful for the unexpected.
I am grateful for the possibilities I have not yet thought of.

AFFIRMATIONS:
My life is unfolding beautifully.
Things are better than I imagine.
Amazing things are happening.
My current situation is leading me to my dreams.
I experience everything at the perfect time.

MEDITATION

Who we become as a result of meditation is more
important than the time spent in meditation itself.

*When meditating, do not expect something
to happen. Otherwise, you are meditating
on your expectation, and you are not
doing the meditation itself.*

~ Master Choa Kok Sui

MEDITATION

Meditation is so much more than sitting in silence, chanting OM, or uttering a mantra. Meditation creates a space in our constant thought process for something new to emerge. By learning how to quiet the mind, we learn how to increase our awareness of what lies beyond the chatter. A consistent meditation practice can balance many of the never-ending emotions and struggles we face in our lives.

Some people initially experience meditation as a series of unwanted thoughts speaking up and making noise the moment they try to experience silence. When they struggle with their thoughts, though, they are actually creating more chatter. The focus of meditation should be more about increasing awareness than emptying the mind. When we become aware of our thoughts, feelings, reactions, body, and breath, awareness expands and grows.

Instead of struggling with thoughts, our awareness of the thinking process creates detachment and disengages our emotions, allowing us to better appreciate the silence and stillness. Awareness is more than just the absence of thoughts.

As the emotions ease and the body relaxes into silence, the mind begins to calm down and eventually becomes still. As we experience inner stillness, the unconscious mind and the inner world can come to life. As your meditation practice develops, awareness expands, and transformation can take place. New ideas can begin to emerge, along with unique thoughts, different sensations, new insights, and fresh clarity.

It might take time, but as our practice develops our meditations give us peaceful, joyful moments that we can enjoy. Some people experience profound love, bliss, oneness, and remarkable healings during meditation. Some develop an amplified ability to think with greater clarity and intuition. These deep internal experiences often develop and begin to express themselves in our active daily life. When the experiences we have in meditation begin to affect our interactions with the world, we begin to bridge the two worlds. That is why who we become as a result of our meditations is more important than the depths we reach while meditating, although the two can seem to mirror each other.

Rule 21
Meditation is like the wind.

In meditation, we just need to be aware. Whatever comes, let it come. Whatever stays, let it stay. And whatever goes, let it go. Be aware of the gentle breeze of inner stillness; experience the essence of the thoughts and feelings that are leaving and the thoughts and feelings that are emerging. The gifts we receive in meditation can come in the form of a gentle image, a sudden insight, a revelation, or a whisper of our higher soul. Treat meditation like the gentle breeze of the wind. Just be aware.

Rule 22
It is through giving that we receive.

Master Choa Kok Sui's Meditation on Twin Hearts begins with a blessing. In it, we give Mother Earth all that we want to receive. By giving first, we become karmically entitled to receiving the blessings ourselves. When the meditation is finished, it is best to take a few moments to bless whatever situation you are working through. Ask for the best outcome for all involved. Imagine a positive outcome, full of happiness for all. We plant the seeds to receive in that which we first give.

Rule 23
Maintain your meditation practice.

We will always have distractions and excuses for not honoring our time for meditation and inner stillness. When life gets stressful or when greater challenges emerge, it becomes even more important than ever to honor our designated meditation times. Find a group, create a practice, and be consistent. The small addition of a consistent meditation practice can make a significant shift in your life. The consistency creates stability for the days we miss our practice. But even on a busy day, remember, it is better to do a short meditation than no meditation at all.

Rule 24
Meditation sensitizes our brains to higher impressions.

Numerous studies have shown that meditation can calm the mind and nervous system, thereby supporting overall health and well-being. Recent research on the Meditation on Twin Hearts has shown that it increases gamma brain waves in regular meditators, resulting in higher sensitization of the brain, clarity, greater focus and intuition, and an enhanced ability to be "in the zone." With daily meditation practice, these energies become a part of daily life creating a consistent mindset of greater clarity and focus.

Rule 25
Meditation raises and expands one's consciousness.

Deep meditation can bring you an experience of pure awareness. This awareness begins to appear within the consciousness. Beyond the limitations of the mind's thought processes, it rises in vibration through our detachment and expands as it reaches higher levels of divine states. It begins in a state of mind in which there is no thinking, but can expand to a place of spirit, or seat of your soul. It is the place of your creative self, your inner knowing, a place where you can listen to the wisdom of your pure self. It is the place of interconnection, harmony, and oneness with all.

INNER REFLECTION & FIRM RESOLUTION:
Reflect:
- Do you have any negative thoughts or beliefs about the practice of meditation?
- What negative thoughts and feelings arise during meditation?
- What are the excuses or issues you face when you want to meditate?

Erase:
- Any negative thoughts and feelings you hold about meditation or the practice of meditating.
- Any issues that come up while meditating or interfering with your ability to relax.
- Any resistance you have to maintaining a regular meditation practice.

Visualize:
- Peaceful, fulfilling meditations.
- Creating time and space for quiet solitude.
- A positive experience to replace the negative thoughts that were erased.

GRATITUDES:
I am grateful for my time of meditation.
I am grateful that people honor the time I need in meditation.
I am grateful for all of my moments of stillness.
I am grateful for my inner growth.
I am grateful for my deep inner experiences of silence and stillness.

AFFIRMATIONS:
The time I spend in meditation is strengthening my mind for other activities.
Meditation is a time for me to re-charge.
I am worthy of my time of self-care and self-love.
My meditation practice nurtures and heals me.
I always have enough time for all I need.

THOUGHTS

The quality of our thoughts determines the quality of our lives.
All words, emotions, and actions begin with our thoughts.

There is a voice that doesn't use words.
Listen.

~ Rumi

THOUGHTS

Our perspectives on life weigh heavily on the thoughts we think. We might not even be aware of all the thoughts we have because they flow through our minds as the dialog through which we see the world. The commentary on our life experience is simply the thoughts we think. If we have negative thoughts, we will most likely see life in a negative way. If we have positive thoughts, the way we see the world will be positive. Our thoughts are our filters, and they need to be examined so that we can proceed in life with the progress we want to make.

Most people would prefer to think positively – but changing one's thinking from negative to positive can be tricky. How can we use our own thoughts to alter the very thing we are trying to change? We might find ourselves in a loop of justifying perspectives, not making the progress we had wanted.

Creating new patterns is an essential part of breaking old ones. We need to stop the patterns of negative thinking while simultaneously creating new, positive ones.

Consider a person who is angry. Anger might be evident in several areas of their life, and it might be present in most of their thoughts, feelings, and actions. In order to break the pattern of being angry, they need to bring an infusion of awareness. They might not realize they have anger, and they might not see the need for a new way of thinking. Usually what's needed is a jarring situation that breaks the pattern or a startling realization that brings greater clarity and snaps people out of their cycles of thinking.

When we embark on a journey of increasing our awareness, we gain insights into our patterns, many of which we might not even be aware of.

There are techniques people use to snap out of patterns and break these kinds of repetitive cycles of thinking. Meditation is a gentle and highly effective way to increase awareness in many areas of life. As our practice grows, awareness of our thoughts and feelings also grows. Awareness is the space created between our usual emotional and mental patterns and the new thinking patterns we want to create. That space gives us the ability to ask ourselves: Are these the thoughts I want to think? Are these the feelings I want to feel? Are these other people's beliefs or my own? Did I take on these opinions from others, or do I really believe this?

Awareness is the space between who we are and who we want to be. As we engage in this space of becoming, we are walking on sacred ground. All things are possible when we create space for something new because we are creating from our unlimited potential.

Bring awareness to your thoughts and watch your thoughts transform. Create space between your thoughts and words, between your thoughts and your feelings, and between your thoughts and actions. Watch how this creates room for new opportunities to engage with intention. The quality of your thoughts determines the quality of your life. All our words, emotions, and actions begin with our thoughts.

Rule 26
Thoughts have energy.

Our thoughts carry a charge, and the more we think them, the stronger they can get. Scientists have discovered that repetitive thoughts form neuronal pathways, and the more a particular thought or belief is activated and reinforced, the stronger the neural pathways become. As we increase our positive thinking, we increase the energy of our positive thought patterns. The ability to control our thoughts is a precious gift that we need to practice. Especially when emotions and thoughts are heightened, the ability to strengthen our minds becomes more important than ever. Master how to think and how not to think and you will begin to practice the art and science of manifesting the life you desire.

Rule 27
How you see the world is a reflection of your thoughts.

"We are what we think." We view the world through the commentary of our thoughts. If we have negative thoughts, we will see the world tinged with negativity. If we have positive thoughts, we will see the world colored with positivity, hope, and happiness. Between the inner and outer reality is space, a gap that provides continuity between the two. That gap gives you the freedom to master your thoughts in accordance with your values and beliefs. If you find yourself feeling as though you are surrounded by negative people, negative situations, and negative experiences, you might want to turn your awareness within and begin changing your views before attempting to change the world around you. This fertile void is the space for you to create the life you desire.

Rule 28
Life is a mirror that shows us what is within.

Times of change can be tumultuous and bring forth mixed emotions. We are often faced with situations that we are not used to facing. Unfamiliar thoughts, repressed emotions, fears, anger, and frustrations might come to the surface unexpectedly and feel foreign. You might even be in denial of your situation because of these emotions. Life is like a mirror, and during trying times, we often see parts of ourselves that we have not seen before. This is a blessing. Have compassion for yourself and understand that these aspects of yourself are emerging for healing and awareness. Stay calm, be aware, and continue to align with your growth.

Rule 29
Over-complaining can create victims.

Notice if you hear yourself in a constant state of complaining. The energy of the negative situation is becoming stronger than the energy of your desire to move forward and take action. It can sometimes be healthy to talk and process through negative emotions, but you don't want to stay in that mindset forever. We must take responsibility for our situation, focus our thoughts and actions towards our desired outcome, and move forward with purpose and will. Complaining weakens our minds and our ability to make good decisions. Be positive! Be proactive!

Rule 30
Criticism is a reflection of negative emotions.

The root cause of criticism comes from negative emotions and thoughts, which stem from our distorted expectations of how others should behave. No matter what happens, we need to be in control of how our reactions are expressed. Being overly critical of other people simply reflects a weakness or insecurity within ourselves. The greatest remedy for intense emotions is to delay them, let them pass, sleep on them, and do self-inner reflection. Try to identify and address the issues within yourself before you externalize them onto others. This wisdom has been repeated and mastered by scholars and great spiritual teachers in every century and in every country throughout time.

INNER REFLECTION & FIRM RESOLUTION:

Reflect:
- What negative thoughts are troubling you?
- How do your dominant thoughts make you feel?
- Ideally, how would you like your thoughts to be?

Erase:
- Any negative thoughts and feelings that you think or feel regularly.
- Any thoughts or experiences that regularly come up that evoke a negative reaction within.
- Any thoughts that bring forth a pessimistic or judgmental viewpoint.

Visualize:
- Happy thoughts creating positive feelings within.
- Loving thoughts and feelings aligned to nurture your heart's desires.
- A positive balance to the negative thoughts that were erased.

GRATITUDES:

I am grateful for all of my positive thoughts.
I am grateful my mind allows me to properly express myself.
I am grateful my mind shares images of love and peace.
I am in harmony with my thoughts.
I am grateful for my mind.

AFFIRMATIONS:

I focus on positive thoughts that support me in my forward movement.
My good thoughts highlight my good qualities.
I think positive thoughts that support and nurture my well-being.
I focus on that which supports my growth.
I feel what I focus on, so I focus on what feels good.

GRATITUDE

When we live in a state of gratitude, our hearts open, our minds seek out the positive, and we become a magnet for all that we appreciate.

Wear gratitude like a cloak, and it will feed every corner of your life.

~ Rumi

GRATITUDE

Jalal ad-Din Rumi suggests that if we only say one prayer a day, let it be "Thank You." We might not be aware of it at times, but life is unfolding for our best interest. It might not be the comfort and ease that we desire, but it is for our highest level of growth and evolution. To be in a constant state of gratitude helps us to align with this higher understanding and unfolding of our lives. Living in a state of gratitude helps to align us with higher vibrations of life, such as grace, love, and compassion.

Gratitude helps us appreciate what we have and helps us see that it is more than enough. When we live in a state of gratitude, our hearts open, our minds seek out the positive, and we become a magnet for all that we appreciate. Goodness will begin to flow to us because we see and feel better all around. Our minds will calm down, and the criticisms will lessen as our hearts expand with more understanding, compassion, and tolerance.

What we focus on tends to grow. This is the magic of gratitude. You might have experienced a hardship such as a loss of work. You could sit at home focusing on "I don't have enough money. It was wrong for them to fire me." And "It was unfair and unjust." These thoughts, however, will shrink your energy and close your heart. It will negatively impact your emotional center and activate your victim mentality. Your energy will become weaker and weaker and attract negative thoughts that are similar to what you are thinking.

Yet even under the same circumstances, you could focus on what has gone right. "I am grateful for the experience of working there, the people and connections I made, and the knowledge I gained. I trust I will find more work and possibly a job I enjoy more for equal or more pay."

Gratitude changes our experience even when the experience itself does not change. If you want a better life, shift your mindset to one of gratitude, and you will soon go from a mindset of "not enough" and "too hard" to realizing you have all that you need and more. Gratitude can create a magnetic quality within your personality and attract all that you want in life.

When we feel grateful for all that we have, we create pathways for more of that to come our way. We attract back to us what we are most grateful for.

If you need more money, be grateful for the money you have, and that will attract more to you. If you want better health, be grateful for the health you currently have, and that will expand and grow. If you crave more love in your life, seek out and feel grateful for all of the love that you feel, and it will grow and attract more back to you. Other people will feel this positive energy and will be drawn into the good vibes.

We enjoy life more when we live in a positive state, believing that things are going well. We will feel happy and pleased with events and people. Our life experience is richer when we appreciate and have gratitude for all that we have. Gratitude begins with a switch in mindset and re-focusing our perspective. Give yourself the gift of seeing the positive in your life; with gratitude, it will begin to overflow to those around you. Gratitude settles and resides in the heart, where all the magic happens.

The Lord Buddha sums up gratitude this way: "Let us arise and be thankful. For if we didn't learn a lot, at least we learned a little, and if we didn't learn a little, at least we didn't get sick, and if we got sick, at least we didn't die; so let us all be thankful." Gratitude is an essential key to happiness in life.

Rule 31
Small gratitudes add up to a big heart.

Start anywhere, anytime, with anything, or anyone. Do not make gratitude complicated. You do not need a special journal or a new pen to begin your gratitude practice. Be grateful for this word, your ability to read, your ability to purchase this book. Feel grateful that you can see. That you can hold this book in your hands. Be grateful you have a desire to make your life better, be grateful for the air you breathe and the chair you are sitting on. Don't wait to be grateful. Small gratitudes turn what we already have into a great abundance. Start small, start somewhere, and start now.

Rule 32
Gratitude is a muscle that must be worked in order to be strong.

As with our thought patterns, what we think consistently will be the easiest for us to connect with when we are in a difficult situation. If we often feel irritated, that will be the easiest emotion for us to feel in challenging situations. It is the same with gratitude. When we build the mental and emotional muscle of gratitude, it becomes easier for us to experience the feeling of being grateful in other situations as well. We want this muscle to be strong, so even when things become challenging, we have the strength to still seek out the positive aspects and find the silver lining — no matter how challenging it might be.

Rule 33
That which ails you becomes your medicine.

When we grow in gratitude, we can begin to tackle even more challenging situations. Gratitude can slowly chip away at some of our deepest hurts and resentments, leaving in their place healing and increased compassion. You might know some people or situations that seem impossible to find anything remotely close to feeling grateful for. These are the very things we should begin to explore with our gratitude. Our greatest pains can turn into our greatest gifts when we shift the negative to the positive. Start small, start somewhere, and start now.

Rule 34
Gratitude opens the door to true forgiveness.

Some people can forgive and forget easily. Some people can remain stuck in their thoughts and feelings for a lifetime. Gratitude offers us an opportunity to soften the edges of our limiting beliefs. As our feelings begin to open our hearts, we find our ability to forgive even the most challenging person, group of people, or situations. Choosing not to forgive hurts us more than them. Forgiveness is a gift we give ourselves to release the negative emotions caused by previous experiences. Gratitude and forgiveness will create more space for the positive aspects of life.

Rule 35
Practice gratitude for action and inaction.

Having gratitude for all experiences — not just the ones we desire — builds gratitude for all of life. Be happy when things work out, as the experience is an expression of Divine Guidance. Yet also be open and grateful when things do not go your way, as it might be a form of Divine Protection. We assume things should unfold as we wish, but unexpected events can bring greater outcomes than the ones we thought we wanted. You will see amazing things happen in your life when you practice gratitude without attachment. Missing an exit might have prevented an accident, for example.

Being late a few minutes might have averted a mishap, and a canceled flight might give you a better opportunity to meet an unexpected person. Cultivate gratitude for everything that happens and for the goodness that something bad did not happen.

INNER REFLECTION & FIRM RESOLUTION:

Reflect:
- What do you feel the most negative about?
- Where in your life do you feel like a victim or vulnerable to others?
- How do you feel like life is unfair right now?

Erase:
- Any negative thoughts and feelings that you think or feel regularly.
- Any thoughts that make you feel victimized or taken advantage of.
- Any ungrateful thoughts and feelings of entitlement or injustice.

Visualize:
- Thoughts that create positive, grateful feelings within.
- Seeing the best in all people and all situations.
- A positive balance to the negative thoughts that were erased.

GRATITUDES:

I am grateful for love, life, and happiness.
I am grateful for this book.
I am grateful for my growth and healing.
I am grateful for the small and large blessings.
I am grateful for everything I have in my life.

AFFIRMATIONS:

Every day I find new things to be grateful for.
I am grateful for every breath I take.
With every step I take, I feel more gratitude.
I am grateful for every experience.
My life is a blessing.

STABILITY

Our inner state should not waiver, regardless
of the happenings in the outer world.

Be like a tree and let the dead leaves fall.

~ Rumi

STABILITY

S tability comes as a result of consistency. We usually feel a sense of stability when events around us are consistent, repetitive, and routine. Our minds, emotions, thoughts, and feelings feel comfortable when similar actions and events occur. We know how to react, we know how we feel about them, and we are more likely to feel safe in our external and internal worlds. Some people call it their "comfort zone."

As we go through periods of change and growth, our comfort zones change. Significant opportunities for growth can present themselves, such as new events, new feelings, and new things that stimulate us, but they can also be unsettling because they are unfamiliar.

We usually seek comfort in what is familiar. We engage in activities that will bring a calming, soothing effect within us, whether spending time with a friend, enjoying a meal with family, or practice of yoga or meditation. We are creatures of habit and take part in familiar activities to bring consistency and stability within.

How do we find a sense of stability during times of change? How do we remain balanced when the world feels out of balance? How do we stay calm when our emotions are being stirred? How do we stay steady when the winds of change come and the path suddenly becomes bumpy?

What if we were able to create stability regardless of the external circumstances? An ultimate goal is to create an inner world that is stable and consistent enough to endure any changes or breaks in our external circumstances.

It is possible to build an inner state to be a place of strength that will not waiver, regardless of the happenings of the outer world. How can we do this? When it comes to our physical bodies, if we keep a steady practice that builds strength, we'll maintain that strength even if we take a break from the habit for a short period of time. Similarly, if we build our internal "muscles" of clarity, peace, calmness, non-reaction, non-judgment, optimism, and focus, we'll be able to maintain them even if there is a break in our normal patterns or cycles.

To achieve it, we begin by developing a stable mindset. We do that by engaging in practices that engage our inner strengths: meditation, yoga, exercise, service, journaling, creativity, and time in nature. The clarity we experience during such times isn't temporary; it's a mindset we can develop to maintain peace within, regardless of what happens around us. Build your inner muscles, and you will stay strong regardless of the outer circumstances.

Rule 36
Start with your strengths.

Start creating your stable foundation on an existing strength. You will have the confidence and muscle memory in your system that supports success in this area. Maybe it is religion, spiritual practice, meditation, yoga, exercise, eating healthy, friendships, getting out in nature, or your work. Begin with this area and proceed with confidence. Start with your strengths; doing so will build a strong foundation for forward movement in other areas as well. When you feel stability growing, move onto another area of interest.

Rule 37
Keep it simple but strong.

Master Choa said, "Break one arrow at a time." We might be overwhelmed by changes that are happening. Don't take on too much at once. Stay focused and strong and, in the areas that are most important to you, keep it simple. Doing too much at once can overwhelm the system and set back our confidence. Once you have created stability in one area, tackle other areas and proceed from there.

Rule 38
Surround yourself with good people.

As we shift and progress in our lives, we might find that our circles of friends naturally begin to change. As our mindsets shift, people we once related to can suddenly seem very different. It is natural to outgrow aspects of ourselves, and that will be mirrored in outgrowing our friends as well. That's why it becomes important to seek out the company of positive people to help with our growth and forward movement. Friendships should support us in our forward movement, not hinder it, so we seek out and surround ourselves with good people. Good people will do good things; this is the environment in which we need to grow.

Rule 39
Build stability within, and you will always walk on stable ground.

When we find ourselves on an unfamiliar, bumpy road, it is more important than ever to find stability within. If we're ungrounded, we can be easily swayed by the fear, uncertainties, and negative emotions around us. But when we are grounded in ourselves, it is easier to remain calm and steady no matter what situation we face. As we familiarize ourselves within, it can become the foundation from which we consistently function, no matter what situation we encounter.

Rule 40
Storms will pass, yet our ability to weather them remains.

We all go through challenges, and at times, we feel like we are being consumed by what is happening to us. Such times can be disorienting as they can uproot long-standing beliefs and ways of being and thinking. The experience might feel as if this will last forever. But, by the law of cycles, the storms will inevitably pass yet the ability to navigate them will remain with us. We might discover new strengths, focus, and determination that we did not have before. When we weather a storm, a new day will come, and we will have grown in the process. That growth is the true gift and meaning of the storm itself.

INNER REFLECTION & FIRM RESOLUTION:
Reflect:
- What areas of my life am I currently feeling overwhelmed or ungrounded?
- Am I taking on too much? What is necessary, and what is unnecessary?
- Am I feeling overwhelmed and unstable from external or internal stimuli?

Erase:
- Any negative thoughts or feelings that are overwhelming.
- Any unrealistic external and internal pressures.
- Any limiting beliefs that make you feel small or stuck in other people's expectations of you.

Visualize:
- Encouraging, positive thoughts that help you feel grounded and stable.

- Consistent, steady actions that create calm, nurturing thoughts and feelings.
- A positive balance to the negative thoughts that were erased.

GRATITUDES:

I am grateful for inner strength.
I am grateful for the confidence to know what is right for me.
I am grateful for the stability I have in my life.
I am grateful for knowing this storm will eventually pass.
I am grateful for this opportunity for growth.

AFFIRMATIONS:

Where I am is exactly where I need to be.
I am stable. I am strong.
I take on what I can handle.
I prioritize my health and well-being.
I engage in actions that create balance and harmony in my life.

RESILIENCE

If we persevere and embrace life's circumstances, we are embracing the inner growth we need to move forward and continue on our journey.

*If all you can do is crawl,
start crawling.*

~ Rumi

RESILIENCE

R esilience is our ability to endure, persevere, and grow regardless of the circumstances of our lives. Movies are made and books are written about people who embody resilience to a high degree. The tremendous strength of the human spirit to look life's struggles in the eye, to stand up after being thrown down, and to stay focused on a goal regardless of the obstacles that we encounter leaves most of us in awe. It is not what we overcome but our ability to overcome it that leaves us speechless.

The outer obstacles we face are merely a mirror reflecting the inner obstacle we must overcome. What might seem difficult to one person can seem very easy to another and vice versa. A triathlon would be a huge undertaking for one person, but for someone that bikes, runs, and swims often, it would not be. When we view something as challenging in life, it is rarely the event itself but rather our view of the event. Are we capable of accomplishing this task? If the answer is No, what aspect of ourselves needs to grow in order to accomplish it?

This is how life is a mirror: external obstacles show us where we need to grow internally to meet the challenges we face.

Each of us embodies resilience to some degree. If we experience an illness, we might struggle to recover, but we eventually regain our strength and get back to normalcy. When we are at the end of a relationship, we might get emotionally overwhelmed for a while, but most of us usually recover, move on, and love again. Financial hardships can be devastating, but they rarely impact us forever as new avenues of building ourselves back up often emerge. In the midst of change or times of uncertainty, we might feel like all hope is lost, but somehow, we regain our faith, build our strength, and move forward toward something different but similar at the same time.

Stories of resilience teach us just how powerful we can be in enduring life's hardships. When Nelson Mandela was jailed for 27 years, he did not buckle under the weight of life's circumstances. He not only transformed himself, he transformed his prison guards and much of the world through his positive mindset, his tremendous compassion, and the power of his resilience. J.K. Rowling, when she was a homeless, single mom, lived in her car, enduring the rejection of numerous publishers before she amassed fame and fortune through her Harry Potter book series.

These stories ignite hope and possibilities because we have all faced situations that felt bigger than us. We all know the feeling when the weight of the world is upon us, and we just don't know if we can persevere. These powerful stories don't just demonstrate that we can endure; they show that on the other side of our obstacles awaits tremendous success.

The obstacles we face shine a light upon the things we need to focus on in order to continue forward. If we buckle and retreat, we lose the opportunity for advancement. If we persevere and embrace life's circumstances, we embrace the inner growth needed to move forward and continue on our journey. And on the other side of our obstacles is where our greatest treasures are waiting, beyond what we had ever thought to be attainable.

Rule 41
We conquer ourselves, not the obstacle.

We tend to get overwhelmed with life situations that we cannot handle. It is not the situation but our reaction to it that we are uncomfortable with. All obstacles are actually opportunities for us to grow and transform. When we go through life's challenges, we have an opportunity to expand our ability to heal and adapt to a new way of being. If we cannot take on new ideas, adventures, or changes, we deny ourselves a way to adapt and grow. It is through the process of living and navigating new experiences that we evolve. It is important to not always focus on the barriers we face but on the qualities we need to develop as we move through them.

Rule 42
Unwavering resilience is rooted in faith.

Unwavering resilience happens when your inner resolve is greater than any external force. People who embody unwavering resilience tend to be fearless overachievers and highly motivated. Nothing can get in their way or inhibit their forward movement. They create, adjust, and maneuver any situation for the best possible outcome. They don't hesitate to step forward into the unknown and do so with confidence. Their comfort zone lies deep within themselves, and it is unshakeable. Their deeply rooted faith and belief that all will work out to their highest good – helps them maintain that level of confidence. They see through the lens of deep faith – that life supports all that they need and want.

Rule 43
Greater purpose helps us prevail.

We tend to invest more effort and focus when we are contributing to something bigger than ourselves, something beyond ourselves. If we focus on larger goals or plans, it pulls us forward, past our discomforts, to the greater outcome. For example, someone might be more willing to run a marathon to raise money for cancer than they would for the joy of running alone. For many, it is easier to endure tremendous hardships for someone else's good or for something bigger than themselves. When life is overwhelming, it helps to focus higher. It shifts your perspective onto something greater, which inspires you to keep moving forward on your journey.

Rule 44
Live with love in your heart, and growth becomes a gift.

In order to truly embrace growth, we need to be open to unexpected changes and adapt to life's unforeseen circumstances. If we fear growth and withdraw, we will find ourselves withdrawing from life itself. When we connect with and live with love in our hearts, we will not only be at peace with ourselves, we will have a more peaceful, loving experience of living. Connecting with love within softens the growth process as we allow and accept whatever arises as part of our journey. No matter what the situation is, growth becomes a gift if we live with love in our hearts.

Rule 45
Focus on your strengths and just keep moving forward.

You might not be sure of each step as you continue to move your life forward, especially when you're overwhelmed and bogged down with big changes. That's OK. Just keep moving forward. Focus on your strengths and take one step at a time. During the process, new emotions that you were previously unaware might emerge, such as a new inner strength, an unwavering dedication to a greater purpose, or an inner drive of some sort. They help you through it. Whatever you do, stay strong, and keep moving forward.

INNER REFLECTION & FIRM RESOLUTION:

Reflect:
- When was I able to face and withstand difficulties in my life?
- In what areas am I dedicated to the outcome more than the process?
- What are my greatest strengths and weaknesses as I move forward?

Erase:
- Any thoughts or feelings that are holding you back.
- Any negative thoughts or feelings that positive outcomes are not possible.
- Any doubts, worries, or fears that life will not support you in all that you need.

Visualize:
- A major success story in your life, including overcoming and accomplishing all of your obstacles and achieving your desired outcomes.
- Life supporting you in every way you need.
- Your inner strength, growing to meet any external obstacle.

GRATITUDES:

I am grateful for my ability to persevere through any obstacle.
I am grateful for my unwavering focus on what I want to accomplish.
I am grateful for all that I have overcome to be where I am today.
I am grateful for people who support me in who I am and what I believe in.
I am grounded and trust my abilities to move forward.

AFFIRMATIONS:

Life supports me in all that I need.
Everything will turn out for my best interest.
I have the ability to move through any obstacle and achieve my dreams.
The universe will open the right doors for me as I walk forward.
I am resilient. I am strong. I am able to create the life I desire.

FORGIVENESS

Forgiving others is a gift you give yourself because
it frees you of the burden of negative emotions.

*Out beyond ideas of wrongdoing
and rightdoing, there is a field.
I will meet you there.*

~ Rumi

FORGIVENESS

Forgiveness has more to do with us than it does with anyone else. Perhaps we have been hurt, betrayed, lied to, taken advantage of, or treated badly, and the pain and anger becomes overwhelming and all-consuming. When we feel emotions like these, we often hold onto the hurt or withdraw, feeling unable to connect fully with life. The pain is in control, not us, and we get lost in our emotional reactions. Our emotions can disrupt our physical health, especially when we harbor them for long periods of time.

Forgiveness involves consciously taking the time to release held feelings of resentment and hurt in order to find peace and reconciliation with a person, event, or situation. It might require an ongoing practice of consistently forgiving and releasing the emotions until they weaken in intensity and can be fully reconciled. If you wonder why you'd want to spend so much time on someone who you strongly dislike, remember that forgiving others is a gift you give yourself. It frees you of the burden of your negative emotions. The process will lead you to a deeper understanding of your pain and the situation, which will help you grow.

Forgiveness is a process; it cannot be expected to happen right away. We experience events in our lives so we can learn the lessons we need to learn. We gain clarity as our emotions calm down, and our minds begin to connect the dots as to why it's happened in the first place. What you learn helps you come to a place of acceptance and peace.

As you develop inner strength and gain clarity, you recognize that you make mistakes, too, and need forgiveness from others, while other people make mistakes, and they require your forgiveness. This process is an essential part of life. It can be very deep and challenging, so it requires a certain amount of growth and development on our part to implement it.

Here's a good place to start forgiving: Imagine in your mind's eye the person you need to forgive. Say to that image: "I forgive you, and I ask for your forgiveness. I bless you, and I ask for your blessings. I love you and ask for your love." Practice this regularly. This simple act of opening communication within ourselves can begin to release and dissipate any heavy emotions we hold.

Forgiveness is a choice. It is an act that you need to consciously engage in and repeat as many times as necessary until you no longer hold any resentment or negative emotions toward the person or situation. If you do it consistently for 30 days, you will experience significant shifts in your emotions and mindset.

So, begin to release and forgive. Love binds people together, but so does anger. If you are unable to resolve your emotions, they will continue to cycle until you can. Break the cycle now. Forgiveness can transform you into a better person, a better soul, and release you from the karmic lessons of your emotions and relationships.

Rule 46
Mistakes are part of life. Learn from them.

When it comes to mistakes, it might be comforting to remember that everyone makes them. Recognizing your errors and taking full responsibility for them – even if it feels uncomfortable to do so – is your first step toward forgiving yourself for your mistakes. Like everyone else, you've also hurt others in your life, so you need to ask others for forgiveness and reconciliation as well. Our teacher has given us these wise words on the subject: "Evolution implies time, process, and a lot of mistakes. Mistakes are part of life. Do not make a big fuss when you make a mistake. Just keep going. Do not be too hard on yourself. Forgive. Forget. And continue to live. Keep the lesson and move on."

Rule 47
Letting go of the past propels you forward.

In the shadows of pain, forgiveness is not always easy, yet an essential part of being able to move forward is to let go of the past. When our minds and emotions are strongly connected to past events, it becomes difficult for us to be in the present and open to new opportunities. When we release resentment and pain, we create space within, and we have more energy that leads us forward, guiding us to create more of what we want in life. Let go of the past. Then, you can move forward with grace and clarity.

Rule 48
Love binds. So does hate.

Love binds, bridges, links, and threads our hearts with someone we deeply love. Hatred, too, can bind us together – just as intensely – with somebody for whom we have strong negative feelings. Through forgiveness, we can transform or disconnect this kind of negative bond. Otherwise, we will continue to experience the hurt we've endured with that person and with others at some point in the future. Practicing forgiveness releases the resentment or vengeance we hold toward those who've harmed us and prevents the reoccurrence of the situation in the future. It releases us and others so we can finally be free.

Rule 49
Self-forgiveness leads to greater empowerment.

Self-forgiveness is essential to creating a strong foundation for our well-being. Many of us carry deep-seated pain from the past, such as shame, guilt, and feelings of regret. These emotions are heavy and toxic to our well-being, so how can we feel good about ourselves when we are plagued with them? Self-forgiveness helps us release the pain we carry and replace it with positive thoughts and feelings from the lessons we've learned from the experiences that created them. This inner transformation will lift the weights of our past and infuse us with the strength and power we need to help us move forward.

Rule 50
Inner forgiveness for all; outer forgiveness for some.

Inner forgiveness is the deliberate act of healing and releasing deep-seated emotions towards someone who has hurt us. Inner forgiveness can be practiced in all situations, no matter how grievous; ultimately, it is the gift of peace we give ourselves. This inner work does not justify others' behaviors, but it is a way for us to be at peace with ourselves and with life. Outer forgiveness is different because we practice it on a case-by-case basis. Outer forgiveness is the process of mending and healing the actual relationship with that person, group, or action. For example, if a friend has done some terrible act that hurt you deeply, inner forgiveness helps you heal your emotions towards that person. On the other hand, if you heal the friendship and remain friends, it is outer forgiveness. Inner forgiveness has to do with love and compassion; outer forgiveness has to do with the necessity to create order and justice. Inner forgiveness for all; outer forgiveness for some. These two must be balanced.

INNER REFLECTION & FIRM RESOLUTION:

Reflect:
- Who has hurt me in the past? What are the circumstances? How long have I been harboring this hurt? Months? Years? 1-5 years? 10-20? Or more?
- Whom have I hurt? What are the circumstances?
- What areas of my life need self-forgiveness?

Erase:
- Any negative thoughts and feelings of anger, hatred toward others, groups, or situations.
- Any negative thoughts and emotions of pain, shame, and guilt toward yourself.
- Any patterns of being a victim.

Visualize:
- Reconciliation and harmony in your relationships and life.
- Past hurts healed and released.
- Your life without emotional and mental baggage of the past.

GRATITUDES:

I am grateful for my ability to forgive.
I am grateful to the people who have forgiven me.
I am grateful to be free of my past.
I am grateful that my relationships are harmonious.
I am grateful for my growth and healing as a result of forgiving others.

AFFIRMATIONS:

I am open to forgiveness.
Every day is a fresh start. Today I choose to forgive.
Forgiving others is a gift I give myself.
The more I forgive, the more I grow.
I am blessed with a loving heart.

SUCCESS

Success is not so much about achieving your goal as it is about
the process and growth you experience getting there.

You've seen my descent. Now watch my rising.

~ Rumi

SUCCESS

Success means different things to different people depending on the goals they're seeking and their ability to actually enjoy accomplishing them. Some people might achieve great things but fail to see themselves as successful, while others can find a great sense of accomplishment in the smallest of tasks. One person might feel like earning thousands of dollars is a huge success; billionaires might not. Some people see fame, fortune, and beauty as markers for success, while some see happiness, inner peace, love, and contribution as the definition of success.

Success can arise spontaneously, but sometimes it needs to be brought forth. The more we focus on all of the successes in our lives, the more we will feel accomplished, motivated, and inspired to do more. The more capable we feel due to accomplishing our goals, the more we will be inspired to continue to move forward. If we consistently feel as though we are failing, our sense of drive will diminish because we will never feel capable. Focusing on our successes builds our confidence and increases our desire to continue to make progress.

It is important to celebrate our progress as we move through uncertain times by acknowledging the smaller milestones. When we find ourselves on the other side of a major journey or a major shift of transformation, there is success. It might not have been what we were expecting or wanting, but as we take a moment to catch our breath and observe how far we've come, there is success. It is important to not fixate on physical outcomes, especially ones that might be outside of our control, but look closer to see some of the smaller internal milestones and pat ourselves on the back for our progress.

Ultimately, success is not based on external events but on the internal satisfaction of achieving a certain goal. Celebrate the process of becoming the person you've become as you achieve your goals, rather than the specific goals themselves. Set small goals and milestones that will help you build your confidence and encourage forward movement to larger goals and successes. If you overwhelm yourself with too many tasks and unrealistic expectations, you are bound to feel like a failure. It becomes a self-fulfilling cycle that will lead to burnout, resentment, and reduced confidence.

True success is more about the qualities we gain by becoming the person who has achieved a desired outcome than it is about the outcome itself. Many achieve goals and will still feel empty; true success is when we accomplish our goals and have a sense of fulfillment in who we are becoming and the sense of contribution our actions had. As we develop and grow, we need to honor the becoming of who we are and our new capabilities to accomplish the goals we originally set out to do. This celebration connects us to living a successful life and instilling in ourselves a mindset that we are capable of accomplishing even greater things. The gift of success is not what we accomplish but who we become in the process.

Rule 51
Align your goals heart to head.

Choose your goals wisely. Goals conceived in the mind alone, such as earning a certain amount of money, might push us forward but, upon completion, leave us feeling empty. On the other hand, some heart-centered goals, such as ending poverty, might be inspiring, but they also might be unrealistic, leaving us feeling inadequate and hopeless when we try to achieve them. It's best to set goals that align with who we are, what impact we want to have (heart), and what we want to accomplish in life (head). It is the connection of heart and head that calls forth our greatest successes because we align our desires with our ability and skills to achieve goals that support who we are, contribute to the world, and express our true selves.

Rule 52
Celebrate each step.

As you begin any journey, celebrate your small steps. Take your larger goal and break it down into manageable steps for realistic forward movement. As you make progress, make sure to celebrate the small milestones along your path, not just the final outcomes. The more successful you feel, the more your desire builds to do more. Celebrate even the smallest of milestones as they all contribute to the final destination.

Rule 53
Know your "Why."

Your "why" is the essence or heart of your goal. When we know our "why," we tap into the beat or pulse of what it is we long to create. It connects us to the meaning and driving force that creates and manifests what we want. Our "why" tends to be connected to our desires and yearnings to create or build something new. Understanding this will ultimately be the force that keeps us going when we begin to feel like giving up. Nietzsche said, "He who has a 'why' can endure any 'how.'" Your "why" is your fuel for moving forward.

Rule 54
Hold the vision and trust the process.

Flow like water around obstacles and adapt to surroundings as you continue toward your desired destination. Life rarely happens as we plan; we need to adapt and adjust according to unexpected circumstances outside of our control. This is part of life. Learning to maneuver our path with ease and grace around life's circumstances is part of our dedication to following through with our goals. If we give up easily when faced with a challenging detour, it shows our lack of dedication to the goal itself. Keep your eyes focused on the end result and trust the process of navigating unexpected changes along the way. Quite often the growth we experience during the journey is preparing us for when we reach the final goal itself.

Rule 55
Emulate those who have achieved what you want to accomplish.

Seek out inspiration from people who live and celebrate what you are working toward. You can learn from their style and mannerisms and emulate the qualities that make them successful. If there is an area that you want to excel in, use that person's techniques and teachings to help you move forward. Learning from their wisdom can help you avoid unnecessary mistakes and help you move forward faster, with greater ease, and with their learned wisdom. Many famous men and women have shown that their success on the outside mirrors the many journeys they took on the inside. Seek out mentors and other people to help inspire you and motivate you toward the goals you desire.

INNER REFLECTION & FIRM RESOLUTION:

Reflect:
- What negative experiences might be blocking your view of success?
- Do you hold resentment toward others?
- What negative thoughts or emotions do you have about where you are now?

Erase:
- Any negative thoughts and emotions you have about yourself in relation to success.
- Any judgment or bitterness you hold toward others.
- Any distorted or negative beliefs you have about success.

Visualize:
- Positive things about your current situation and your ability to move forward toward your goals.
- Experiences that positively balance out the negative thoughts you erased.
- Visualize yourself as successful and fulfilled.

GRATITUDES:

I am grateful for the success of my journey.
I am grateful for all of my new strength, clarity, and appreciation for everything I learned.
I am grateful for my new mindset and perspective.
I am grateful for my joys and infinite blessings.
I am grateful for all my successes, big and small.

AFFIRMATIONS:

My life is a blessing, and I have everything I need.
My life is full and abundant with all of life's gifts.
I am successful, fulfilled, and happy in everything that I do.
I am grateful for the blessings of my process.
Everything is turning out in perfect order.

REFLECTION

Reflection is when we look back over our journey so far and paint a silver lining around all of our experiences, helping us to learn the lessons and celebrate the seen and unseen gifts.

*The desire to know your own soul
will end all other desires.*

~ Rumi

REFLECTION

The Silver Lining

L ife is happening for us, not to us. This minor change in wording offers a massive change in our perception. Life is a gift, and the things that happen to us, as challenging as they might be, happen for our benefit. Even if we are in pain or wrestling with our struggles, if we can find a silver lining to our situation, we are in a better position to nurture our growth and spiritual development than if we feel resentful that things didn't go the way we wanted.

We don't usually see the positives of a challenging time until it has passed. For example, if we are moving to a new home, the process can be exhausting and overwhelming, but when we look back, we often see that our new location, new neighbors, and friends make it all worthwhile.

Reflection is when we look back over our journey so far and paint a silver lining around all of our actions, helping us to instill within ourselves the lessons from our experiences.

Without reflection, we might continue to hold bitterness or resentment for past events that were challenging. But when we look for a silver lining, we can infuse the lessons and positive energy they give us into our challenging and overwhelming experiences. Reflection, especially when we seek the good in what has occurred, can be very healing. We can assess why things happened and how we have grown because of them. And we can transform our mindset from one that was negative to one filled with gratitude for the experience.

Seek the silver lining in all that you do. If you look back and cannot find the silver lining, you might still be in the process of healing and transformation. Keep the intention, and, at some point, you will find the gift within the uncertainty; you will know that you are better because of the experience.

Rule 56
The silver lining is seen through the heart.

When we see the world from a victim's perspective, we can't see the silver lining. When we shift our mindset to one of gratitude, we can suddenly appreciate and learn from challenging times. If you are stuck thinking, "I can't believe this happened to me," your mind will be filled with heavy thoughts and feelings, and a silver lining won't be within view. Shifting your thinking to one of gratitude opens your heart and eyes to find the gift of the struggles you've faced. Each of us must find a strong footing to step out of the role of victimhood. Life is happening for our benefit. No matter how difficult it might be to see the silver lining, it is there.

Rule 57
There is always a gift.

Behind every challenge in life, there is a gift. As difficult as it might be, under the surface, we still heal, grow, and learn from what we experience on the surface of things. Even with a broken heart, sickness, loss, or financial struggle, there are still gifts waiting to emerge. We must seek the positive side effects, the new friendships, and the unexpected turn of events and allow our minds to appreciate the unexpected. The mind can get overwhelmed with all that went wrong, so try to redirect your focus onto what is going right, even if there is also pain or sorrow. Focus on the gift; there are always gifts.

Rule 58
Change up your view.

If you are feeling stuck, playing with other perspectives can help shift you. Zooming out, looking within, projecting your vision to look forward, and looking back in reflection can help unlock a stuck perspective. Ten years from now, things might look very different. Look at it physically, emotionally, and mentally – and look at it from others' viewpoints, too. Being able to look at your life with a bird's eye view will offer a greater perspective of your life and the interplaying experiences. You can even go deeper and attempt to see it from your soul's perspective. Keep looking until the silver lining begins to emerge.

Rule 59
Where there is one gift, there will be more.

If you can get one positive thought out of a negative situation, take it and build on it. Elaborate, expand, and draw it out. As you do, you will find even more to appreciate. The sun was shining, you made new friends, and you learned something new about yourself. You had no idea how strong you were; you learned to do things differently; you made new connections, started a new project, or met a new community. Where there is one gift, appreciate it, and it will multiply.

Rule 60
Turn the situation inside out.

Focus on the silver lining so much that the whole situation eventually turns itself inside out, and you see more positive aspects to the situation than negative ones. That is the ultimate healing. When we can transform our life experiences so that they support our growth and evolution, we begin to face situations knowing there is a gift – and the whole journey is transformed as you go forward in life with an open heart. We seek the good, overlook the struggle, and find the silver linings within it, no matter how challenging.

INNER REFLECTION & FIRM RESOLUTION:

Reflect:
- Where do you still hold negative thoughts and emotions from your past?
- What situations do you remember as having no gifts or no silver lining?
- In what ways does dark thinking still pull you down, overwhelming you with negativity?

Erase:
- Negative viewpoints, negative thoughts, and feelings.
- Any feelings of victimhood.
- Any resentment towards others in a given situation.

Visualize:
- Encouraging, positive thoughts that help you feel grounded and stable.
- Consistent, steady actions that create calm, nurturing thoughts and feelings.
- A positive balance to the negative thoughts that were erased.

GRATITUDES:

I am grateful for my internal strength.
I am grateful for the confidence to know what is right for me.
I am grateful for the positive and good things in my life.
I am grateful for all of the lessons I have learned so far.
I am grateful to be exactly where I am in life.

AFFIRMATIONS:

I have faith and trust that where I am and who I am are exactly where I need to be.
I am stable. I am strong.
I prioritize my well-being.
I create balance and harmony in my life.
Life is supporting me in all ways.

TRANSFORMATION

Transformation is the process of evolving to
a greater depth of the truth in ourselves.

*You transform all who are touched by you.
Mundane concerns, troubles, and
sorrows dissolve in your presence.*

~ Rumi

TRANSFORMATION

Transformation is alchemy; you create something new from something not yet that. You can experience change without transformation, such as when you move to a foreign city. In that case, you might find yourself in a completely new environment while you remain exactly the same inside. Transformation, on the other hand, requires adaptation, learning, growing, and becoming more of yourself. Learning a new language, trying new practices, meeting new people, and taking in new perspectives can contribute to transforming yourself.

Your inner world benefits from transformation more than your outer world. Change is travel; transformation is who you become because of your travels. Change is an external event that happens to you; transformation is an internal process of development and evolution.

Consider a situation involving ending a relationship or divorcing. While the physical separation is the change, the transformation would be reflected in the healing, growth, and clarity that come from the experience. Or consider seeing someone you haven't seen in years and noticing that they are exactly the same. You might even say to them, "You haven't changed a bit!" Clearly, in the years that have passed, the person has experienced changes of some sort, but they have not transformed. They are still thinking, behaving, and acting the same. On the other hand, someone might go on a spiritual retreat and transform their emotions, mindset, and perspectives of life in a very short time.

Our awareness of our transformation is the very thing that defines our "spiritual path." We could be wandering aimlessly from one experience, one relationship, or one job to the next while still not embracing the inner alchemy of life. Transformation helps us grow and evolve to a higher level of being. On our spiritual path, transformation can be a guiding force that helps us through the challenging times that we might otherwise find difficult to comprehend. Knowing the inner world is alchemizing; we can trust the process even if we do not yet see the results.

When we transform, we reach a greater depth of truth within ourselves. Transformation brings us closer to who we really are as we peel off layers of distorted thinking and reveal greater clarity. Our rigid thoughts and feelings can be transformed to be softer and encompass more understanding. When we have anger, we can transform it into love. When we are jealous, we can transform it into support and encouragement. Whatever we experience that is in conflict with parts of ourselves and the world, we can transform. Alchemy begins as energy is infused into whatever is resistant to transformation.

Some people consider the benefits of transformation to be the meaning and purpose of life; they will seek and celebrate the gifts that transformation brings even more than the experience itself. When faced with a highly stressful situation, they open themselves, allowing the experience to deeply trigger their emotions and negative thinking so they can lean back, with awareness, and let the experience itself purify them. By detaching and aligning with a higher mindset, the process can help us release our negative emotions, and the experience becomes secondary to the goal of transformation.

Transformation involves looking deeper than what we are experiencing and focusing on the process of becoming more of ourselves. It might be an internal process, but we will see the benefits in the outer world. Situations or events that used to be stressful will become more harmonious; our hard thinking will become softer; judgments and criticism will decrease; we will have more compassion and tolerance for others. Life softens as we transform.

Rule 61
Embrace the questions.

As human beings, we tend to value the answers more than the questions and the solution more than the problem. For the most part, we live in a "quick-fix" world. As we embark on the journey of transformation, we need to begin to embrace the process, which involves embracing certain questions that arise. When we engage in these steps instead of always focusing on the result, we naturally open to a greater awareness than only solitary solutions. We move from our linear mindset and begin to see new possibilities. Transformation is about creating something that is not yet in existence. To support it, we need to engage the mind in thoughts and feelings that widen the limits of our thinking. So, we embrace the questions.

Rule 62
The way out is to go within.

Transformation can be challenging and force us to confront some of our strongest beliefs and feelings. We might find ourselves feeling like we want "out," we are done, and we want to walk away from the process. After all, it can get intense! The way for us to "get out" is to go within, that is, not within the mind but within the heart. Let the mind rest and begin to explore some of the sensations and feelings within your emotions and your body. The mind tends to override with logic and direction, but when the mind reaches its limit of capacity, tune into the wisdom of your heart for a reprieve.

Rule 63
Fear is an illusion.

Our fears limit us. They suppress our thoughts and actions, limiting their range of functionality to what we would normally call our "comfort zone." During times of transformation, we often get pressed up against the boundaries of our comfort zone, feeling as if our sense of reality is being challenged. Fear itself is an illusion, a projection of the worst-case scenario into the future. Acknowledging this illusion helps us to re-establish ourselves in the foundation of the moment and choose our thoughts and feelings differently. When we are fully present, fear dissolves, and other opportunities open up.

Rule 64
Always transform up!

Always make sure that you are transforming in a good and positive direction for yourself. Especially when you are overwhelmed or run down, be sure to keep your thoughts, feelings, and intentions aligned with a high vibration in order to guide the transformation process towards progress and growth. Be more aware of your feelings and your actions as they are indicators and reflections of what is happening within. If you feel yourself slipping downward, lift yourself and focus on more positive, affirming perspectives to turn yourself around.

Rule 65
Wrap yourself up in that which you want.

Like a caterpillar that wraps itself up in a cocoon, surround yourself with what you want to create. If you want to be more positive, loving, kind, and compassionate, surround yourself with thoughts, feelings, people, books, movies, and programs that reflect what you want to create. Your life and your experiences should symbolize the cocoon in which you transform. Your friends, environment, books you read, and clothes you wear are reflections of your inner state. Surround yourself with that which you want to create.

INNER REFLECTION & FIRM RESOLUTION:
Reflect:
- What areas of my life still bear the scars of pain or hurt? Where do I still find resentment and internal bruises from past situations?
- What within me is still not healed? When thinking about it, what events still stir up emotions?
- What situation or people bring forth unsettled feelings and thoughts?

Erase:
- Negative feelings towards yourself or others from situations about which you hold feelings of bitterness.
- Any feelings reflecting a victim mentality.
- Any limiting beliefs that make you feel small and stuck in other's actions towards you.

Visualize:
- Possible gifts from situations that used to feel negative.
- Stronger emotions, actions, and feelings arising because of the situation.
- A positive balance to the negative thoughts that were erased.

GRATITUDES:
I am grateful for my increased awareness.
I am grateful for the spiritual muscle of transforming my struggles into my strengths.
I am grateful for the unexpected gifts I have found in my life.
I am grateful for all of my blessings.
I am grateful for new eyes that see a deeper truth.

AFFIRMATIONS:
My life is full of blessings.
All opportunities are unfolding for my highest good.
My life is full of unexpected gifts.
I find strength as I grow through my struggles.
I embrace transformation and keep my eyes open to the blessings that come with it.

MOVING FORWARD

Moving forward is a natural process.
The journey of our lives is one of movement.

*As you start to walk on the way,
the way appears.*

~ Rumi

MOVING FORWARD

To move forward in life, we must fully accept our current situation. Things might not be as we want them to be or how we planned them to be; either way, complete acceptance gives us a stable foundation to move forward. It is an opportunity to reflect and process the journey we're on and to prepare ourselves to forge ahead and create something new.

Acceptance involves completely letting go of the past and the events that led up to it. We can't continue to struggle with what has happened in the past and expect to create something new going forward. If we want to proceed with a positive self-image and confidence in what is to come, we need to embrace all the events that brought us to where we are now.

In moving forward, it's always good to start with a plan, no matter how vague it is. What is your desire? What is most important to you right now? What is a must for you? Narrow in on what is essential and begin to give it structure with your imagination. If your heart's desires were to materialize, use your creative energy to map it out and bring life to your dreams. Be as clear as possible with your intentions and your vision. The degree to which you can see it with clarity is the degree to which the universe can respond and help you create it.

Every day, write down your vision, thoughts, reflections, and goals. This daily journal will become your roadmap as well as your reminder of why you are embarking on the journey you've chosen.

Aligning with your vision is necessary; it will begin to generate feelings and desires for what the outcome might be like. We do not always attract what we want; we attract what we are. The ability to imagine the life we desire will attract and draw in that very thing. Envision it and feel it in all the senses. As it becomes more and more real within us, it will begin to materialize in the external world.

To create anything, we need energy; energy is the force of creation. So it's important to keep your energy high as much as possible. Start simple. Exercise, eat healthy foods, spend time with positive people, create a daily meditation practice, make time for avenues of creativity that inspire you, and do service to help those in need. As your energy builds, deeper meaning and purpose will begin to surface.

We can connect to the depths of life by connecting to the depths of ourselves. People spend so much time trying to find their life purpose or seek a deeper meaning. But if you practice right thoughts, right words, and right actions, they will fill your life, giving you a sense of purpose and vitality.

Moving forward is a natural process. The journey of our lives is one of movement. Stagnant energy creates problems, just as stagnant water becomes a swamp. It's stuck. We want to move forward like a river instead – flowing, adapting, adjusting, and creating new pathways. When we move ahead on our journey, we are living, trying again, and creating something new.

Whatever it is that we seek in the world outside of us, we can first create within through our thoughts, feelings, and beliefs. As we flow in our river of life, we will continue to build momentum, and we will grow and develop. Life is a journey; we are meant to keep moving forward.

Rule 66
Acceptance is being at peace with how things have turned out.

Acceptance aligns with stability. The degree of acceptance we hold equals the degree of our faith. Acceptance doesn't just come to us when our desired outcome arrives. We are in full acceptance when we trust that things have turned out exactly as they should. Wherever we lack acceptance, we lack faith, thinking things should have been different. Trusting that everything has unfolded exactly as it should have creates a solid foundation for us to move forward into the future. We can't be whole, happy, and confident at the same time that we're angry and upset with our lives. With acceptance, we find peace with what is.

Rule 67
Act from intention, not expectation.

If the actions we take are based on other people's expectations, we will constantly feel overwhelmed and underappreciated. This is true for many people, although they might not realize it. We often dress, speak, and act based on the reactions we expect to get from the people closest to us – not grounded in our authentic and true selves. Take time to get clear about what you want and what you need to get done. Meet your own expectations and your own desires. People-pleasing is exhausting and overwhelming, and it is the quickest way to get off track from living your purpose. Act from internal intention, not external expectations.

Rule 68
Not all routes will be shown on your roadmap.

Journeys rarely unfold as we expect them to. So what's the value in planning? Planning actually helps us become aware of our expectations and gets us thinking and focusing on where we need to go and what we need to do. It's very helpful to begin the process with a clear plan of events and an expected destination. Be aware that most trips don't end up following the plan exactly, so we can remain open to alternate routes if they become necessary. Having an idea of where we are headed helps us align our minds and emotions with that outcome. The trip might change, but the destinations should remain. Hold the vision. Trust the process.

Rule 69
Daydreaming helps solidify the vision.

Daydreaming is a wonderful way to energize your goals. Spend time thinking and daydreaming about the life you envision. Visualize it. Feel it. Play it out in your mind. Your senses will come alive when you align with those daydreams. Make a movie in your mind's eye and live the beauty of what it would be like to live your dream. This will open your heart, activate your senses, and expand your mind. You will begin to experience your goals as a present reality, and your energy will begin to match that frequency and draw it closer to you.

Rule 70
Always keep your energy high.

You might have many good intentions, goals, and dreams, but if you do not have enough energy, you will not be able to manifest those into a reality. Energy is the fuel of life. Low energy leads to low output; high energy leads to high output. If you keep your energy high, you will be able to start new things and follow your dreams – and still have energy for your family, your friends, and things you love. A person with high energy will not get as overwhelmed due to a busy schedule; they'll have adequate fuel to implement, navigate, and adjust as necessary. Keeping your energy high is an essential part of moving forward. If life is like going on a road trip, keeping your energy high is like keeping a full tank of gas. You are not going to go very far if you are low on fuel. It is the same with energy. Energy is everything.

INNER REFLECTION & FIRM RESOLUTION:

Reflect:
- What fears do I hold about the future?
- What thoughts are holding me back from dreaming big?
- Where do I feel overwhelmed and held back by life?

Erase:
- Any regrets that you still hold from the past.
- Thoughts that contain you and make you feel stuck.
- Any fears that the future will have the same patterns as the past.

Visualize:
- The life you are dreaming of.
- Being happy in your life.
- Being full of energy, physically, emotionally, and mentally.

GRATITUDES:

I am grateful for my ideas and visions.
I am grateful I have desires and dreams.
I am grateful I can think big.
I am grateful for all of the support I receive.
I am grateful I have a plan for my future.

AFFIRMATIONS:

I attract everything I need in life.
I fulfill my dreams.
My plans are clear and focused.
I have the energy to fulfill my dreams.
I love my life!

10 GOLDEN RULES
for a GOOD LIFE

Be present and celebrate the moments that make you feel the most alive. Allow life to pulse through you and experience the magnificence of our human existence. Be one with God as energy effortlessly flows through your whole being. Recognize the formless beauty of who you really are and how invaluable your precious time on this Earth is.

Everything in the universe is within you. Ask everything of yourself.

~ *Rumi*

10 GOLDEN RULES
for a GOOD LIFE

Some rules stand alone, not needing a context to be powerful, and we consider the following ten rules to be so. They can be applied to any person, to any phase, and to any given situation. They are universal truths, tried and true, that can be called on at any time for guidance on your path. They can be tremendously helpful to grounding yourself in a good, wholesome, successful, and fulfilled life.

Golden Rule 1
Trust the wisdom of your heart.

When faced with a question, a dilemma, or uncertainty, tune into your heart and ask, "What does my heart say?" The response often comes as a gentle inner knowing, and your trust in it will grow. When you align from the heart, you begin with love and this invisible force will guide you forward. Love is the true foundation of all great things we want to build in our lives. By following the wisdom in your heart, you honor its infinite wisdom and unbiased guidance. *Tune in and listen.*

Golden Rule 2
Take good care of your soul's vessel.

As we work with rules and guidelines to help us move forward in life, we must not forget the physical form that we embody. We can grow, heal, transform, and succeed, but if our physical body is not healthy, strong, and vibrant, we will not be able to experience the true joys of a life well-lived. Our physical health is essential to living a vibrant life. When we are healthy and strong, the mind is clear, the body is full of energy, and we have a strong form to contain all of our hopes, aspirations, and dreams. The way there does not have to be complicated – eat real food, spend time outdoors in nature, exercise, and focus on your well-being. The stronger our physical bodies are, the more energy we have and the more we can accomplish in life. *The physical body is your temple; treat it well.*

Golden Rule 3
Forgive. Forget. And move forward.

Our ability to forgive ourselves and others correlates directly with our ability to move forward and grow. You cannot evolve emotionally or spiritually while you hold onto heavy resentments. It might take a short amount of time, or it might be a lengthy process. Regardless, it is worth every second you spend on it. If you do not neutralize the hurts you hold in this lifetime, you will most likely face them again and again until you do. Release the burdens that hold you down and cut the strings pulling you back. *Forgive easily, forget quickly, and keep moving forward.*

Golden Rule 4
Do service and tithe.

Our teacher, Master Choa, has left us this wisdom as a pillar of our spiritual practice. If you want to improve your life, which we all do, then be in service to help others. Tithe to charitable, philanthropic, and spiritual organizations that are making the world a better place. As we lift others up, we generate good karma that lifts us up, too. Tithing is like planting seeds – what you plant will grow and come back to you. If you donate food, an abundance of food will come back to you. If you donate money, an abundance of money will come back to you. If you want to have a good life in the future, plant the seeds of a good life now. Service and tithing are avenues to improve your life and generate good karma to move forward with grace and ease. *If your life is difficult, this practice is essential.*

Golden Rule 5
Be aware of thoughts that divide.

The goal for mankind is ultimately to align with our higher souls and become more harmonious in our collective existence. It might seem like an insurmountable task, but we can start with our own thoughts. All words and actions towards others originate as thoughts in our minds. Be aware of thoughts that divide you from others. When you find yourself having feelings that are separative, divisive, or judgmental, be aware of them, recognize them, and try to find the right viewpoint before they manifest. These kinds of negative energies create more distance between us and others. Attempt to see other perspectives, insights, and other possibilities to neutralize the intensity of the issue within first. *Global change begins with each one of us.*

Golden Rule 6
Being authentic takes courage.

We live in a world that can overwhelm us with pressure to become something other than who we are. Our consumerist culture actively tries to persuade us, promising happiness, if we acquire certain things, make certain decisions, and engage in certain behaviors. It takes great courage to be fully honest and open to expressing yourself in alignment with who you are and how you feel instead of being the way others expect you to be.

It is important to remind ourselves that life is not always meant to be perfect and full of sunshine. Being authentic is allowing whatever truth you feel within to be the place you function from. Having the courage to be authentic is a radical act in today's world; still, more and more people are doing just that. They are breaking through society's expectations and speaking up for their truth. *Be authentic and emanate the courage to be true to yourself.*

Golden Rule 7
Align your life with purpose.

Many successful people accomplish amazing things but still feel empty inside. Living a life of purpose fills our lives with meaning and substance. Each person's purpose is unique to them and cannot be projected on others. To find your purpose, look for what makes you feel the most alive. People who live aligned with purpose say that when they "work," time disappears, physical needs vanish, and they become engrossed in the moment. There is a natural energy that arises when you love what you do.

It's great if your purpose aligns with your career, but it's also OK if it doesn't. Still, you should do what you love most as much as possible. When you feel the most alive, you experience a sense of peace, contentment, and fulfillment with who you are and how you spend your time. *Engage in activities that make you feel the most aligned, and you will slowly start living your life's purpose.*

Golden Rule 8
When life becomes too much, ask for help.

When life becomes too overwhelming for you, please reach out to someone who can help. Seek the support of others. In this human experience, we are meant to help and love each other. When the burden gets too heavy, seek out support from your partner, family, friends, an advisor, therapist, or a certified pranic healer. If we wear a facade of "Everything is OK," even when it's not, it isolates us and pushes others away. We are all hurting in some way, yet we are meant to come together to support each other's growth. There is no shame in being human; we are meant to help each other through our life experience. We create stronger bonds and connections when we do. In our most vulnerable times, we connect with others most authentically when we speak the truth of what we are honestly experiencing. *We gain strength when we ask for help.*

Golden Rule 9
Do not believe everything you are taught.

Our teacher, Master Choa, said: "Do not believe blindly. Use intelligent evaluation to draw your own conclusions." Information and knowledge are available in great abundance today, but we cannot believe everything we read or see. Come up with your own truth through active analysis of the data you learn. What is true for one person might not be true for another. So, engage with the rules in this guide to discover deeper truths for you and your life. Then, we encourage you to design your own rules and guiding lessons. Do not believe everything you are taught. *Draw your own conclusions intelligently – based on your own life experience.*

Golden Rule 10
Trust in a force greater than yourself.

By trusting a guiding force greater than yourself, you automatically lift yourself upward and forward. If we stay isolated in our thinking, we might end up cycling through the same thoughts and ideas over and over. But a force greater than ourselves can help pull us out of feeling stuck or lacking confidence in our ability to make it through. Some people connect with God, religion, spirituality, or a spiritual teacher. Some might connect with a mentor, parent, or successful person. Focusing on a greater force inspires us and gives us hope that we can make it and that we are destined to succeed. *Trust in something higher than yourself.*

AFTERWORD

Regardless of what kind of uncertainty you are experiencing, it will certainly not be the only challenging situation you will ever encounter in life. Change is an inevitable and essential part of life. Our intention for these guiding rules is to help you navigate uncertain times with greater ease while reaping as many benefits as possible.

As a well-experienced world traveler gains lessons along their journey, the journey itself offers gifts to help navigate future travels with greater ease. As you feel more prepared to face life's challenges and obstacles, you might find yourself reviewing these Rules. Each time you do, you'll gain greater clarity, awareness, strength, and confidence in your ability to move forward in your life, heal, and grow.

You might find certain experiences easier to manage while others still seem like they're pushing you past what you think you can handle. Each phase might be different; each experience might vary. Some rules might stand out more at one time than others. Keep this book close by as a companion to offer guidance, clarity, or greater depth whenever you need it. Read it cover to cover or seek out the parts that help you most when you feel stuck and need guidance to move forward.

The guiding rules we present here are not new in their meaning, just their interpretation. The meanings have been taught, practiced, and mastered by men and women throughout history. Since ancient times, fundamental guidelines on how to better oneself and one's life have been shared by great spiritual teachers, the wisest of men, exalted souls, holy gurus, and holy masters. The rules we share within these pages are our own interpretations as we face today's uncertain times.

While interpretations vary depending upon the time, place, and need, the essence of these ageless teachings remains the same. We invite you to look beyond the rules and find the essence in each one. Ultimately, we encourage you to embrace the paradox that you might need to create your own rules through your own personal interpretations when the need arises.

Our heartfelt wish to you is to just keep moving forward.

Godspeed.

ABOUT THE AUTHORS

Glenn J. Mendoza, M.D.

Is one of just eight Master Pranic Healers in the world and a practicing neonatologist in New York State. He touches the lives of thousands of people worldwide through his inspiring words, deep insights, and joyful character. *Rules That Guide Us* is his sixth book.

www.MasterGlenn.com

Dawn M. Myers

Is a spiritual life coach and Pranic Healer living with her two boys in Atlanta, Georgia. After spending many years transforming her own life, she now loves awakening the magic and possibilities in others through her coaching, energy healing, speaking, and writings. Dawn has also published two children's books.

www.DawnHealerCoach.com

This book is a collection of the rules, insights, and action steps that the authors took on their journey through 2020. Their intention is to spotlight those silver linings — the hope, inspiration, and growth — that we experienced as a group at this unprecedented period of time. These rules can be powerful guideposts for anyone's journey forward.

Books by Glenn J. Mendoza, M.D. and Dawn M. Myers

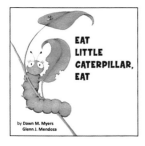

Eat Little Caterpiller, Eat - A beautiful story that infuses magic in the hearts and minds of readers as they embark on a loving journey of transformation. Join our Little Caterpillar as she journeys through her fears, lets go of the past and embraces the good to help her transform and move forward as we are all meant to do! A metaphor and story of inspiration for all ages.

Books by Glenn J. Mendoza, M.D.

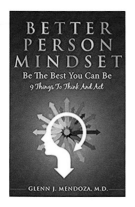

Better Person Mindset - Have you ever asked yourself, "If I know better, I will do better?" If so, the insight and wisdom within these pages will set you on the journey to becoming a better person. We all aspire to become a better person - a better leader, husband, wife, partner, parent, doctor, nurse, healer or teacher. This book discusses the nine paramount principles to facilitate high order thinking which allows you to think clearly, reasonably, rationally and emphatically, properly, and accordingly. Weaving together concepts from enduring spiritual and intellectual traditions with practical suggestions for today's world.

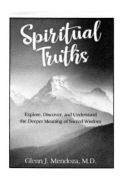

Spiritual Truths - Soul stirring, thought provoking and heart opening, Dr. Glenn Mendoza unveils universal spiritual truths that deepen our understanding and experience of our soul. Through these pages, we discover and explore the meaning of sacred wisdom, awakening our hearts to the innate desire to strengthen our spiritual connection as we experience that very thing between the pages of this profound book. A must read for anyone looking to grow on their spiritual path.

The Real You - The Real You is a remarkable primer to guide people of all ages to look beyond our physical form to see the spiritual truth of who we really are. This book is beautifully displayed with colorful images and simple text to express the inner spiritual teachings simplified for young children, or serve as powerful reminder for adults that we are more than this physical body, we are the soul!

Pushing The Boulder - Powerful parable to remind and inspire Pranic Healers that the vital work of moving healing and spirituality forward depends on a loving heart, a desire to serve, and our deep unwavering faith in the Spiritual Teacher. Read to remember the true purpose of our spiritual work does not always equal the outcome of our actions, but more importantly the growth we experience as we align and set our hearts intentions on a purpose greater than ourselves. A must for anyone on their spiritual path who is longing to make a difference in the world.